NARCISSISTIC PERSONALITY DISORDER TOOLBOX

55 Practical Treatment Techniques for Clients, Their Partners, & Their Children

DANIEL J. FOX, PH.D.

Copyright © 2018 by Daniel J. Fox. *Narcissistic Personality Disorder Toolbox*

Published by:
PESI Publishing & Media
PESI, Inc.
3839 White Ave.
Eau Claire, WI 54703

Cover Design: Amy Rubenzer
Editing: Jenessa Jackson
Layout: Bookmasters and Amy Rubenzer

Printed in the United States of America
ISBN: 9781683731528

PESI
Publishing
& Media

www.publishing.pesi.com

About the Author

DANIEL J. FOX,PH.D., has been treating and specializing in the treatment and assessment of individuals with personality disorders for over 15 years in the state and federal prison system, universities, and private practice. He is a licensed psychologist in the state of Texas and author of *The Clinician's Guide to The Diagnosis and Treatment of Personality Disorders*; the award winning *Antisocial, Borderline, Narcissistic and Histrionic Workbook: Treatment Strategies for Cluster B Personality Disorders*; and several articles on personality, ethics, and neurofeedback.

His specialty areas include personality disorders, ethics, burnout prevention, and emotional intelligence. Dr. Fox has been teaching and supervising students for over 15 years at various universities across the country, some of which include West Virginia University, Texas A&M University, University of Houston, Sam Houston State University, and Florida State University. He is currently a psychologist in the federal prison system, Adjunct Assistant Professor at the University of Houston, and also maintains a private practice that specializes in assessment and working with challenging clients.

Dr. Fox has given numerous workshops and seminars both domestically and internationally on effective treatment of clients with personality disorders, ethics and personality disorders, personality disorders and crime, emotional intelligence, burnout prevention, managing mental health within the prison system, and others.

For more information on Dr. Fox go to his website: www.drdfox.com

This book is dedicated to my three heartbeats:
My wife Lydia and my two children Alexandra and Sebastian

Table of Contents

SECTION 1

TREATING THE CLIENT ALONG THE NARCISSISTIC SPECTRUM

Setting the Stage for Successful Treatment

Addressing and Changing Maladaptive Patterns

Digging Deeper into Motivations and Lessening Symptomatology

Final Steps of Successful Treatment

SECTION 2

TREATING THE PARTNER OF A NARCISSIST

Setting the Stage for Successful Treatment

SECTION 3

TREATING THE IMPACT OF NARCISSISTIC PARENTS

Who this Workbook is for and How to Use it

Narcissism is a treatable condition, whether in a client, as a part of a relationship, or as a family dynamic. Many clinicians feel frustrated and overwhelmed when working with individuals along the narcissistic spectrum, their partners, and with children of narcissistic parents. This workbook is designed to help clinicians assist clients to grow out of the hurt and pain associated with narcissism. Many times these issues feel irreversible, but the truth is that with the right treatments and interventions, changes can be made that move the client, their partners, and their children away from the impact of narcissistic pathology toward healthier and more adaptive functioning.

The worksheets, exercises, and activities in this workbook are specifically designed to help clinicians successfully work with clients along the narcissistic spectrum, partners in a relationship with an individual along the narcissistic spectrum, and/or children of a parent/caregiver along the narcissistic spectrum. Within each client type section (individual, partner, or child) is a specific four-part sequence that is influential when working with individuals with personality disorders – in this case, narcissistic personality disorder or an individual along the narcissistic spectrum. The first part of each section sets the stage for successful treatment, which involves identifying the issues and concerns that are present.

The second section involves addressing and changing maladaptive behavior patterns that keep clients stuck in narcissistic pathology or cause them to remain in a narcissistically influenced relationship with a partner or parent. The third part of each section digs deeper into what motivates clients to continue their narcissistic behavior or to remain in a relationship with an individual along the narcissistic spectrum (this includes children with narcissistic parents). The fourth and final part of each section is composed of steps to finalize successful treatment after reducing the impact of narcissistic pathology by helping clients make better choices for themselves.

THE APPROACH TO THE NARCISSISTIC SPECTRUM AND NPD IN THIS WORKBOOK

In this workbook, the term "along the narcissistic spectrum" will be used to include individuals who exhibit narcissistic traits in varying degrees, as well those who meet criteria for narcissistic personality disorder (NPD).

Section 1

Treating **The Client** Along **The *Narcissistic*** Spectrum

Setting the Stage for Successful Treatment

WHAT ARE YOU DOING HERE?
NARCISSISTS DON'T SEEK TREATMENT

Individuals along the narcissistic spectrum do not come to treatment unless they encounter a narcissistic wound of some kind; this can include being mandated for treatment. A narcissistic wound is a psychological injury that hurts their view of themselves and the world. This injury can be caused by many different factors, such as being threatened or criticized by a significant other, a boss, a family member, or a coworker. It can also result from threats of divorce or abandonment, a failure to achieve a goal, or having been treated in a particular manner by someone that they perceive as valuable.

When individuals along the narcissistic spectrum incur a narcissistic wound, they have to stabilize their view of the world by eradicating the object (e.g., person or situation) that caused the wound. When they cannot eradicate that object, the wound festers, and it is at this time that they come into treatment or are willing to at least attend one session. It is at this time that we, mental health providers, need to assess and make inroads to increase their motivation to attend and participate in treatment. The **Why Are You Here?** worksheet, coming up, is designed for this purpose.

NEXT STEPS

The following worksheet is broken down into three sections. The first section asks clients to identify the presenting problem for which they have sought treatment. This can include being threatened with divorce, being fired, mandated to treatment, or contending with a child who did not attain an unrealistic goal and believing they must "teach" the child to not be "a loser" (their conceptualization). Presenting problems can also include factors associated with incurred narcissistic wounds.

The second section of the worksheet contains different qualities often observed in individuals along the narcissistic spectrum. Clients are asked to rate the degree to which these qualities are important to them on a 10-point scale, with 1 being "not at all important" and 10 being "extremely important." Most of the items in this section are typical aspects related to the expectations held by those along the narcissistic spectrum, except numbers 3, 4, and 8. These exceptions, when rated highly, illustrate that the client may be more open to traditional therapy; the client recognizes that there are issues at hand and is willing to work on areas that need improvement. This is in contrast to the "classic view" that individuals on the narcissistic spectrum want therapy to focus on other problem areas (e.g., the belief that others are not providing them with enough accolades or appreciation of their unique self).

The third section asks clients to operationally define what they want out of therapy and how they will know when and if they have made gains. Because many individuals along the narcissistic spectrum have impaired insight, they tend to be poor judges of realistic goal and success attainment. This final section also aligns the therapist with the client in identifying and providing markers of success. **As therapists, we have to connect with clients along the narcissistic spectrum in order for them to want to pursue therapy and make changes to lessen maladaptive patterns.**

WHY ARE YOU HERE?

I.   Presenting Problem (what brought you into or to consider treatment)**:**

_____

_____

II.   How important are the following aspects to you?

I want to be:	1 = Not at all; 10 = Extremely important									
Recognized for my value	1	2	3	4	5	6	7	8	9	10
More powerful	1	2	3	4	5	6	7	8	9	10
Worth more to others	1	2	3	4	5	6	7	8	9	10
Appreciated	1	2	3	4	5	6	7	8	9	10
More socially influential	1	2	3	4	5	6	7	8	9	10
Not misunderstood	1	2	3	4	5	6	7	8	9	10
Getting what I deserve	1	2	3	4	5	6	7	8	9	10
Less lonely	1	2	3	4	5	6	7	8	9	10
More influential	1	2	3	4	5	6	7	8	9	10
Other:	1	2	3	4	5	6	7	8	9	10

III.   Clearly describe how you will know if therapy will be/has been helpful for you. Clearly describe the behaviors, feelings, and/or thoughts you would like to see changed by participating in therapy.

Goal example: *I will receive higher ratings on my work evaluations, and my coworkers will follow my directions more often and more accurately. I will have to tell them directions fewer times, and they will make fewer errors.*

Goal #1: _____

_____

_____

Goal #2: _____

_____

_____

Goal #3: _____

_____

_____

TO TREAT OR NOT TO TREAT: THE DISTINCTION AND OVERLAP BETWEEN NARCISSISTIC PERSONALITY DISORDER AND ANTISOCIAL PERSONALITY DISORDER

Much has been written about the overlap between narcissistic personality disorder (NPD) and antisocial personality disorder (ASPD) (APA, 2013; Fox, 2013, Kernberg, 1998; Millon, 2011; Ronningstam, 1999, Ronningstam, 2011). For example, individuals on the narcissistic spectrum – particularly those on the extreme end – can present with antisocial and psychopathic features, including purposeful behavior to dominate, humiliate, and manipulate others (Kernberg, 1998; Widiger, 2006). Importantly, individuals with both antisocial and narcissistic traits face greater complications and have a decreased probability of successful treatment outcomes compared to individuals with narcissistic traits alone.

Treatment is further complicated when clients with combined antisocial and narcissistic traits incur a narcissistic wound, causing feelings of shame and humiliation, and potentially leading them to act out in a violent manner in order to restore their sense of narcissistic self-esteem (Gilligan, 1996). These are significant factors that derail the course of treatment and worsen their prognosis. However, even in the absence of antisocial and psychopathic traits, individuals with NPD tend to be treatment rejecting and possess many therapeutic challenges of their own. Therefore, it is imperative that we discern between the two disorders to provide a clear therapeutic picture of these clients and increase their ability to collaborate and participate in treatment.

NPD and ASPD have been called "near neighbors" when the traits are examined clinically and empirically, which adds to the need for distinction between the two (Gunderson & Ronningstam, 2001). Ronningstam (1999 & 2011) makes a distinction between narcissistic traits and antisocial traits in that individuals diagnosed with NPD are typically more grandiose, passive, less aggressive and impulsive, and engage in behaviors to enhance their self-image for the purpose of attaining praise. In contrast, individuals with ASPD tend to be more exploitive, have a less fragile ego, possess a superficial value system, possess an insensitive and cruel disregard for others, perpetually engage in criminal behavior, and focus on material gain or sexual gain. These similarities and differences add to the need for clinicians to distinguish between these two neighboring disorders and the usefulness of the included worksheet.

NEXT STEPS

The next worksheet, **The Antisocial Addition**, is designed to help clinicians make the distinction between these two very separate, but at times similar, personality disorders. It will help you determine if your client along the narcissistic spectrum can collaborate and participate in treatment. The chart is composed of features to distinguish between those who exhibit a combination of antisocial/narcissistic features versus those who exhibit narcissistic features only.

If there are more factors marked in the left column, this indicates a greater likelihood that your client is not a suitable candidate for individual therapy (and possibly group therapy) because of the presence of the antisocial/narcissistic combination. If there are more factors marked in the right column, this indicates a greater likelihood that your client possesses narcissistic features only, and the likelihood of successful treatment outcome and prognosis is increased.

THE ANTISOCIAL ADDITION

ANTISOCIAL/NARCISSISTIC FEATURES	NARCISSISTIC ONLY FEATURES
☐ History of acting out violently when feeling ashamed or humiliated	☐ No history of aggression or deceit
☐ Tends to be indifferent to the welfare of others	☐ Genuine feelings of guilt or remorse after harming or causing harm to another
☐ Evidence of deceit, amorality, and deception in relationships	☐ Identity is based on approval from others
☐ Feels s/he does not need to conform his/her behavior to social norms	☐ Goals are focused on gaining approval from others
☐ When shown the truth, s/he displays an attitude of indifference	☐ Will pay attention to others but only to the extent that it is of relevance to him/herself
☐ Convincingly displays an air of justified innocence	☐ Relationships tend to be superficial and serve his/her self-esteem
☐ History of acting out impulsively	☐ Reluctant to engage in dangerous or risky behaviors
☐ Not highly needy of admiration or envious of others	☐ Intimately restrained due to lack of genuine interest in partner's experience outside of relevance to self
☐ Violent acts are preceded by feelings of shame or humiliation	☐ Emotionally expressive (positive or negative) to get his/her emotional needs met
☐ Meets criteria for conduct disorder: needs at least 3 of the 5 below, before age 15:	☐ Has a history of trusting others and is less suspicious of other's motives
☐ Aggression towards people and animals	☐ Tends to be reactive, as opposed to proactively planning to meet a nefarious goal
☐ Destruction of property	
☐ Theft	
☐ Lies to obtain goods or favors	
☐ Serious rule violations	

QUESTIONNAIRE TO DISTINGUISH BETWEEN ENTITLEMENT AND NARCISSISTIC PERSONALITY DISORDER

Entitlement, as it pertains to a *DSM-5*® diagnosis of NPD, is defined as "unreasonable expectations of especially favorable treatment or automatic compliance with his or her expectations" (APA, 2013, p. 669). Although entitlement is indeed a symptom of NPD, it is often misconstrued in our society to denote the same construct as narcissism. This incorrect assessment can cause mental health providers to see the client as more pathological, challenging, and disruptive than is actually the case.

However, it is much easier to treat a client's sense of entitlement than it is to treat an individual who meets full criteria for NPD because entitlement is just one out of the nine symptoms listed in the DSM-5. The client must exhibit five or more symptoms to qualify for the full diagnosis of NPD. What does this mean for the treatment provider? It means that it is a good sign if your client has only one symptom of the full disorder, given that the more symptoms that are present, the greater the challenge it is to treat and work with this individual.

The next questionnaire will help you distinguish between a sense of entitlement and other components of NPD.

NEXT STEPS

Provide the **Me and My World** questionnaire to your client and ask him/her to fill it out. Once completed, you can calculate the results based upon the scoring table below. Give 1 point for every "Yes" answer. There is no cutoff score to categorically identify "an entitled person" or someone with NPD with this questionnaire. The purpose is to dimensionally determine their propensity toward these traits in order to better understand how they see themselves and their world. As an additional note, the greater the number of narcissistic traits that are identified on this questionnaire (i.e., even numbered questions that are answered "Yes"), the greater the challenge to treatment. The tools provided in this workbook will help you address and change the patterns exhibited by clients characterized by entitlement and narcissism, but we first have to know what issues and factors we, as mental health providers, are contending with.

> **ODD NUMBERED QUESTIONS = ENTITLEMENT CRITERIA**
>
> **EVEN NUMBERED QUESTIONS = NARCISSISTIC CRITERIA**

ME AND MY WORLD

Please indicate "Yes" or "No" to each question. Your therapist will calculate the results and discuss your scores. Please answer as honestly and truthfully as you can.

1. _____ My family, children, friends, acquaintances, lovers, employees, and/or employers must meet my expectations.

2. _____ I expect to be recognized for my superior talents and abilities.

3. _____ I have excessive unhappiness over my troubles, and I let it show.

4. _____ I cannot help but think about my unlimited success, brilliance, beauty, and deserving of ideal love.

5. _____ Others might have to work their way up, but I should not have to.

6. _____ I deserve a lot of respect and admiration for all I do.

7. _____ My happiness is justified, even if it is at the expense of others.

8. _____ I often feel bitter about what other people have or achieve.

9. _____ If others do not do what I want, I will ignore them or scream and yell at them.

10. _____ I have no problem showing people I am better than they are.

11. _____ I have a hard time negotiating or compromising.

12. _____ The only people who really understand me are other "special and unique" people.

13. _____ My needs should be prioritized, even at the expense of others.

14. _____ I have no regrets about other people suffering so that I can succeed.

15. _____ I often upset people by what I do or say.

16. _____ It is not uncommon for me to react with rage or disrespect if I am criticized.

SCORING THE ME AND MY WORLD QUESTIONNAIRE

First, add up all of the even and odd numbered questions that were marked "Yes" in the appropriate boxes below. Then, use the rating scale to determine the degree of entitlement and/or narcissistic characteristics present in your client. This rating will provide you with a reference point in regards to the degree of entitlement and narcissistic traits with which you will be contending throughout the treatment process.

Scores can range from 0 to 8; there are 8 factors related to entitlement and 8 factors related to NPD. Be aware that this is not a diagnostic tool but, rather, is designed to identify the degree to which your client exhibits these traits, which influences the probability of successful treatment.

EVEN NUMBERED "YES" (Entitlement)	ODD NUMBERED "YES" (Narcissistic Traits)

0-2	3-5	6-8
Mild	Moderate	Severe

ENTITLEMENT RATING	NARCISSISTIC TRAITS RATING

IDENTIFYING MILD TO EXTREME FACTORS OF NARCISSISTIC PERSONALITY DISORDER

The field of psychological diagnosis and treatment changed significantly with the publication of the *DSM-5* (APA, 2013). This change has especially impacted how we recognize and address personality disorders with the introduction of an alternative model of personality disorders that is dimensional in nature. Although categorical models have largely dominated the field, dimensional models can also directly benefit treatment plans and treatment approaches by allowing clinicians to better identify and target adaptive and maladaptive characteristics (Livesley, 2007).

Although the personality disorder criteria in the *DSM-5* has remained the same for the last several editions, our approach and conceptualization has changed as a result of the addition of an alternative diagnostic model that characterizes personality disorders in terms of (1) impairments in personality functioning and (2) pathological personality traits. As part of this alternative model, the DSM-5 has provided a dimensional rating system of personality functioning called the Level of Personality Functioning Scale (LPFS). The LPFS allows clinicians to rate the degree of impairment in personality functioning on a scale that ranges from "Little or no impairment" to "Extreme impairment" (APA, 2013, pp. 775-778). Each level in the LPFS is listed in the figure below.

This scale brings the dimensional model to the forefront and helps clinicians recognize the presence or absence of particular challenges that clients bring to the treatment environment. Consider the treatment variance of a client with NPD who has some impairment in entitlement, empathy, and grandiosity compared to an individual with severe impairment in these same areas.

Clients with "some impairment" are likely to participate in treatment, be responsive to feedback, and have a greater degree of insight into how their behavior impacts their life and the lives of those around them. They are also more likely to recognize that by maintaining the belief that they are better than everyone else contributes to their own issues and the issues they have with those around them. Further along the dimension are clients with "severe impairment," who are resistant to attending treatment and lack the insight to recognize how their belief that they deserve special treatment hurts their chances of success. They also exhibit disregard for other's feelings, which further hinders their self-control and motivation to work effectively with others, and they are reluctant to recognize how their self-centeredness and condescension are core issues to examine, change, and improve their life. The prognosis for these two clients are significantly different, as those further along the LPFS are more challenging and have a poorer prognosis for treatment success, as shown below:

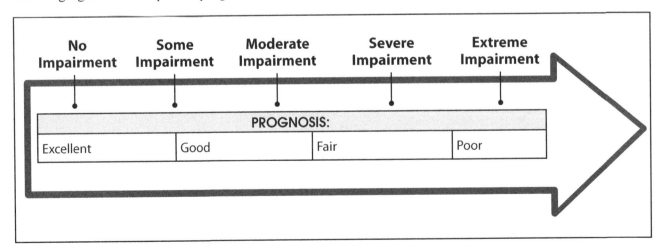

Prognosis identifies the likely course of a psychological disorder. In the case of NPD, the further along the dimension individuals are, the poorer their prognosis because of the greater severity of narcissistic traits. To gain insight into treatment prognosis and better anticipate treatment planning, clinicians need to determine the level of narcissistic traits that are present in their client who falls along the narcissistic dimension and the impact that the expression of those traits will have on the treatment process. The scale on page 10 is designed to help the clinician gain this insight in order to best plan the course of treatment and interventions appropriately.

It is important to note that this activity is not a strict use of the categorical and/or the alternative model of personality disorders in the *DSM-5*, but a combination of the two to apply the best of both to the clinical environment.

NEXT STEPS

The **Narcissistic Expression Scale** is composed of 17 factors related to symptoms of NPD. These factors were derived from the criteria associated with the alternative *DSM-5* model of NPD, as well as the NPD criteria from the International Statistical Classification of Diseases and Related Health Problems (APA, 2013; World Health Organization, 2016). After your client has completed the scale, add up the scores for all 17 items, and use the chart below to determine the degree of narcissistic traits that are present. The higher the score, the more prominent the narcissistic traits, the higher the degree of treatment complexity, and the poorer the prognosis.

It is important to recognize that just because individuals have a fair or poor prognosis, it does not mean that they cannot benefit from treatment. What this typically means is that treatment tends to move at a slower pace, there is likely going to be more resistance, and there is a greater degree of impaired insight.

> **63 – 85 = High degree of narcissistic traits**
>
> **40 – 62 = Moderate degree of narcissistic traits**
>
> **1 – 39 = Low degree of narcissistic traits**
>
> **Pay particular attention to items identified with 4 or 5.**

NARCISSISTIC EXPRESSION SCALE

Circle the degree to which these statements characterize your life. Your therapist will calculate the answers and discuss your scores. Please answer as honestly and truthfully as you can.

1. I define myself by referencing others.

    1 = Never   2 = Rarely   3 = Sometimes   4 = Often   5 = Always

2. I feel more important than anyone else.

    1 = Never   2 = Rarely   3 = Sometimes   4 = Often   5 = Always

3. How I feel about myself determines how well I control my emotions.

    1 = Never   2 = Rarely   3 = Sometimes   4 = Often   5 = Always

4. My goal setting is based upon the degree of approval from others.

    1 = Never   2 = Rarely   3 = Sometimes   4 = Often   5 = Always

5. My standards are very high to show how exceptional I am or so low that they are easily attained.

    1 = Never   2 = Rarely   3 = Sometimes   4 = Often   5 = Always

6. I have difficulty recognizing or acknowledging what motivates me.

    1 = Never   2 = Rarely   3 = Sometimes   4 = Often   5 = Always

7. I have difficulty recognizing the feelings and needs of others.

    1 = Never   2 = Rarely   3 = Sometimes   4 = Often   5 = Always

8. I am overly sensitive to reactions of others but only in terms of how it impacts me.

    1 = Never   2 = Rarely   3 = Sometimes   4 = Often   5 = Always

9. I see myself as highly influential on others.

      1 = Never   2 = Rarely   3 = Sometimes   4 = Often   5 = Always

10. My relationships are designed to make me feel better about myself.

      1 = Never   2 = Rarely   3 = Sometimes   4 = Often   5 = Always

11. I have little interest in other's experiences.

      1 = Never   2 = Rarely   3 = Sometimes   4 = Often   5 = Always

12. I am driven to achieve for myself only.

      1 = Never   2 = Rarely   3 = Sometimes   4 = Often   5 = Always

13. I have absolute right to what I want.

      1 = Never   2 = Rarely   3 = Sometimes   4 = Often   5 = Always

14. I have a high degree of focus on myself and what I am doing.

      1 = Never   2 = Rarely   3 = Sometimes   4 = Often   5 = Always

15. I am better than most or all other people.

      1 = Never   2 = Rarely   3 = Sometimes   4 = Often   5 = Always

16. I have no patience for mistakes.

      1 = Never   2 = Rarely   3 = Sometimes   4 = Often   5 = Always

17. I feel that others are unworthy of my consideration and/or respect.

      1 = Never   2 = Rarely   3 = Sometimes   4 = Often   5 = Always

THE TWO FACES OF NARCISSISM: OVERT AND COVERT

NPD is not a linear construct; no personality disorder is. Viewing NPD as a linear construct oversimplifies the disorder and causes many mental health providers undue stress due to anger, frustration, and a sense of helplessness when working with an individual along the narcissistic spectrum. Many of these feelings are a result of not knowing what type of NPD the clinician is working with. Wink (1991) identified two types of NPD, vulnerability-sensitivity and grandiosity-exhibitionism, which have been supported by research over the last two decades (i.e., Besser & Priel, 2009; Brailovskaia & Bierhoff, 2016; Rose, 2002, Zondag, 2005).

The names have changed, but the concepts have remained the same: vulnerability-sensitivity is now referred to as *covert narcissism*, and grandiosity-exhibitionism is now referred to as *overt narcissism*. Identifying the type of narcissism within the therapeutic environment will help lessen disruption and increase the probability of successful goal attainment. The **Me and The World Around Me** measure presented next is designed for the clinician to help identify if the client fits more into the overt or covert narcissistic domain. It is important to recognize that many individuals along the narcissistic spectrum will have components of both, but typically there is one type that is more central and the other peripheral. A visual representation is provided below:

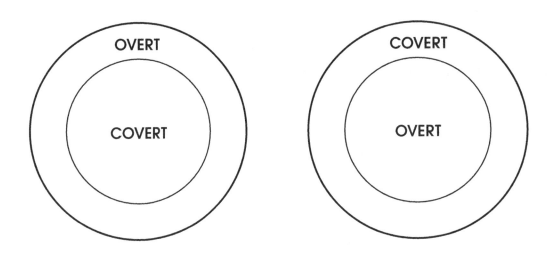

After you have assessed which type is more prominent using the measure below, you can discuss this with your clients and discuss how it adversely impacts their functioning and contributes to their difficulties. In turn, you can design treatment to help them lessen their destructive maladaptive patterns.

Remember to speak in a language that your clients can understand, which includes reminding them that changing their maladaptive patterns will increase their ability to become more socially influential, will give them a greater presence in their relationships, and will enhance their self-control and influence in various situations. Using this language will not exacerbate their narcissism; instead, it will allow them to hear you and clarify how working with you benefits them.

NEXT STEPS

The **Me and The World Around Me** measure on the next page can be taken by you (the mental health provider), from the perspective of your client, or by clients themselves. In some cases, both you and your client can take the measure together to see if you agree on the results. Use the table below to calculate your scores and discern which subtype of narcissism is central and peripheral.

COVERT NARCISSISM: QUESTION NUMBER					
1	2	3	4	9	10
11	12	16	17	18	24
25	26	30			Total:

OVERT NARCISSISM: QUESTION NUMBER					
5	6	7	8	13	14
15	19	20	21	22	27
28	29	31			Total:

Once you have the results, you can use the other tools in this workbook to help you address, manage, and attenuate the narcissistic traits that are causing difficulty for your clients and others.

ME AND THE WORLD AROUND ME

Please circle the number related to each statement that best represents your beliefs, thoughts, and perceptions of yourself and those around you. Answer all questions as honestly as you can.

1. I feel like I am in a lower position than others.

①	②	③	④	⑤
Strongly Agree	Agree	Neither	Disagree	Strongly Disagree

2. I annoy or irritate others with persistent fault-finding or continuous urging.

①	②	③	④	⑤
Strongly Agree	Agree	Neither	Disagree	Strongly Disagree

3. I cannot trust or depend on others.

①	②	③	④	⑤
Strongly Agree	Agree	Neither	Disagree	Strongly Disagree

4. I will change my values if it means someone will like me.

①	②	③	④	⑤
Strongly Agree	Agree	Neither	Disagree	Strongly Disagree

5. I am impressive and magnificent in my appearance or style.

①	②	③	④	⑤
Strongly Agree	Agree	Neither	Disagree	Strongly Disagree

6. I am pleasant and attractive.

①	②	③	④	⑤
Strongly Agree	Agree	Neither	Disagree	Strongly Disagree

7. My relationships are short-term and mean little to me.

①	②	③	④	⑤
Strongly Agree	Agree	Neither	Disagree	Strongly Disagree

8. I make it very clear that I am humble and not too extravagant to gain favor with others.

①	②	③	④	⑤
Strongly Agree	Agree	Neither	Disagree	Strongly Disagree

9. I am unsure of myself and my decisions.

①	②	③	④	⑤
Strongly Agree	Agree	Neither	Disagree	Strongly Disagree

10. I am not committed to any one occupation or employer.

①	②	③	④	⑤
Strongly Agree	Agree	Neither	Disagree	Strongly Disagree

11. I am envious of others' impressive appearance or style.

①	②	③	④	⑤
Strongly Agree	Agree	Neither	Disagree	Strongly Disagree

12. I lie often and cannot help myself.

①	②	③	④	⑤
Strongly Agree	Agree	Neither	Disagree	Strongly Disagree

13. I focus on my dreams of outstanding success.

①	②	③	④	⑤
Strongly Agree	Agree	Neither	Disagree	Strongly Disagree

14. I am successful.

①	②	③	④	⑤
Strongly Agree	Agree	Neither	Disagree	Strongly Disagree

15. My principles of right and wrong behavior and the goodness or badness of human character changes when it suits my needs.

①	②	③	④	⑤
Strongly Agree	Agree	Neither	Disagree	Strongly Disagree

16. I am embarrassed or guilty because of my actions, characteristics, or associations.

①	②	③	④	⑤
Strongly Agree	Agree	Neither	Disagree	Strongly Disagree

17. I have interests in many things, but I do not explore any of them.

①	②	③	④	⑤
Strongly Agree	Agree	Neither	Disagree	Strongly Disagree

18. Other people's boundaries are not a concern of mine.

①	②	③	④	⑤
Strongly Agree	Agree	Neither	Disagree	Strongly Disagree

19. I have a right to what I want.

①	②	③	④	⑤
Strongly Agree	Agree	Neither	Disagree	Strongly Disagree

20. I work hard to attain the admiration of others.

①	②	③	④	⑤
Strongly Agree	Agree	Neither	Disagree	Strongly Disagree

21. I do not care about other people's feelings.

①	②	③	④	⑤
Strongly Agree	Agree	Neither	Disagree	Strongly Disagree

22. I pretend that monetary status is not important to me, when it really is.

①	②	③	④	⑤
Strongly Agree	Agree	Neither	Disagree	Strongly Disagree

23. How I see myself is delicate and vulnerable.

①	②	③	④	⑤
Strongly Agree	Agree	Neither	Disagree	Strongly Disagree

24. I am bored most of the time.

①	②	③	④	⑤
Strongly Agree	Agree	Neither	Disagree	Strongly Disagree

25. I do not care about other people's time and responsibility. My needs come first.

①	②	③	④	⑤
Strongly Agree	Agree	Neither	Disagree	Strongly Disagree

26. Rules and authority figures are not important to me.

①	②	③	④	⑤
Strongly Agree	Agree	Neither	Disagree	Strongly Disagree

27. I appear to be self-sufficient to others.

①	②	③	④	⑤
Strongly Agree	Agree	Neither	Disagree	Strongly Disagree

28. I have a strong desire to achieve my goals.

①	②	③	④	⑤
Strongly Agree	Agree	Neither	Disagree	Strongly Disagree

29. I cannot work in a group setting.

①	②	③	④	⑤
Strongly Agree	Agree	Neither	Disagree	Strongly Disagree

30. I am hurt easily by setback and criticism.

①	②	③	④	⑤
Strongly Agree	Agree	Neither	Disagree	Strongly Disagree

31. My children are more important to me than my significant other because my children are a part of me.

①	②	③	④	⑤
Strongly Agree	Agree	Neither	Disagree	Strongly Disagree

Addressing and Changing Maladaptive Patterns

IDENTIFYING SURFACE AND CORE STRUCTURES OF NARCISSISTIC PERSONALITY DISORDER

When working with individuals along the spectrum of NPD, or any other personality disorder, you have to examine the disorder from a dual framework. This dual framework is composed of a core structure and surface structure. The core structure is the motivating force underneath the surface structure, which comprises manifested behaviors and thoughts. In order to have long-term impact, you must treat the core structure. In order to effectively do this, you have to know what the core structure is. The best way to identify it is to work backwards from the surface structure to the core structure, since the former is easier to identify. The graphic below illustrates this conceptualization by listing common surface structure factors seen in individuals along the narcissistic spectrum, as well as common core structure factors.

SURFACE STRUCTURE (BEHAVIORS/THOUGHTS)

Takes advantage of others to achieve own goals	Reacts to criticism with rage	Excessive feeling of self-importance	Exaggerates achievements and talents	Preoccupied with power and success fantasies

Unreasonable expectations of favorable treatment	Needs constant attention and admiration	Obsessive Self-interest	Pursues mainly selfish goals

CORE STRUCTURE (MOTIVATORS/DRIVING FORCES)

FEAR SHAME GUILT DOUBT INFERIORITY

To illustrate core and surface structure in a client along the narcissistic spectrum, we will discuss Tony. Tony is a client who has a tendency to become very loud and boisterous if others do not agree with him. This has caused him significant difficulties at work, as he has lost many jobs and has problems with his significant other, who has threatened to leave him. After working with Tony for a period of time, he and his therapist were able to pinpoint that he reacts this way out of *fear* (core structure content) of being perceived as foolish and "stupid."

Whereas many therapy hours could be spent focusing on the manifestation of his *fear* across various contexts, therapy is much more beneficial and impactful when focusing on Tony's conceptualization of his *fear* and his reaction and assumptions when his *fear* is triggered. He and his therapist focus on what his *fear* means, its origin, and how he conceptualizes it in different situations with different people. They then work on countering his fear by identifying success, engaging in counter behaviors that promote confidence in his abilities, and enhancing his personal empowerment (see worksheet on The 5 Factors to Enhance Personal Empowerment). This is a simplified example, as many clients along the narcissistic spectrum display multiple surface structure behaviors and thoughts that have many underlying core structures. What this example does is illustrate the benefits and usefulness of using this dual approach to help your clients who fall along the narcissistic spectrum.

NEXT STEPS

The Driving Forces worksheet lists common core structure motivators on the left and common surface structure behaviors and thoughts on the right. Consider your client along the narcissistic spectrum – do you know what his or her core structure is and how it manifests? This activity will help you identify it.

Once you have identified the core structure, you can examine it in treatment, and you will begin to notice that the core structure becomes a theme in your client's life that pervades every facet, including his or her relationships, perceptions, and goals.

THE DRIVING FORCES

Draw a line from the relevant core structure content on the left of the worksheet to the relevant surface structure on the right. The core structure content is likely associated with several surface structure behaviors and thoughts.

CORE STRUCTURE (MOTIVATORS/DRIVING FORCES)	SURFACE STRUCTURE (BEHAVIORS/THOUGHTS)
	Takes advantage of others to achieve own goals
 FEAR	Reacts to criticism with rage
	Excessive feeling of self-importance
 SHAME	Exaggerates achievements and talents
	Preoccupied with power and success fantasies
 GUILT	Unreasonable expectations of favorable treatment
	Needs constant attention and admiration
 DOUBT	Obsessive Self-interest
 INFERIORITY	Pursues mainly selfish goals

IDENTIFYING THE MOTIVATORS TO GIVE UP MALADAPTIVE BEHAVIORS AND BELIEFS

Why do your clients along the narcissistic spectrum not change? Do they not notice that they are the impetus for the majority of their problems? Do they not see that if they adjusted their behavior they would have significantly fewer problems and hurt others less? The answer to all of these questions is "No, they do not," and that is because their maladaptive patterns are too reinforcing, and those maladaptive patterns work to meet their core structure needs that provide them with a sense of psychological safety.

We call this area of psychological safety our "comfort zone." The comfort zone for your clients along the narcissistic spectrum typically includes:

COMFORT ZONE

- Pervasive grandiosity
- Lacks empathy
- Overly sensitive
- Fantasy preoccupation
- "Special" and "unique"
- Requires excessive admiration
- Sense of entitlement
- Interpersonally exploitive
- Envious of others

These clients do not experience dissonance associated with their comfort zone behaviors and beliefs because they work to get their needs met. It is also difficult for them to consider that if they move outside of their comfort zone, then they will achieve many more goals that encourage positive growth in relationships, employment, and physical and mental health. Although these represent the exact things that they want to achieve, doing it differently means operating in a manner that is new and frightening.

What these individuals do not see is that these goals are elusive when they engage in maladaptive comfort zone behaviors. In order to move outside of their maladaptive behaviors and beliefs, they must be motivated to do so, and in order for us to help them as mental health providers, we have to recognize the ever-critical motivating factors that are present. The core structure directly influences motivation, which is the internal and/or external drive that encourages us to act; provides us with the stamina to continue toward our goals; gives us the energy to overcome obstacles, boredom, fatigue, stress, and distraction; and provides us with the resolve to engage in or resist maladaptive and unhealthy patterns. There are four types of motivators: external negative, external positive, internal negative, and internal positive. These are pictured in the quadrants below:

EXTERNAL NEGATIVE	EXTERNAL POSITIVE
INTERNAL NEGATIVE	INTERNAL POSITIVE

Some examples of these different motivating factors are provided in the four quadrants below:

EXTERNAL	Fear Violence Ridicule Inconsistency/Unpredictability Lack of Respect	Encouragement Kindness Patience Empathy Appreciation
INTERNAL	Fear Lack of trust in oneself Insecurity Doubt Loneliness	Determination Love Hope Desire Self-satisfaction
	NEGATIVE	**POSITIVE**

We are all influenced by different internal and external, negative and positive motivators, and your clients along the narcissistic spectrum are no different. As you probably noticed from the four quadrants above, many of your clients have similar motivators. These may even be some of *your* motivators. It is never the motivators that are maladaptive; it is the behavior patterns and beliefs that your clients along the narcissistic spectrum engage in and hold onto that are problematic in their lives and to those around them.

When working with individuals on the narcissistic spectrum, we have to know what their motivators are in order to examine their core structure, influence adaptive behavior change, and help them grow out of their maladaptive behavior patterns and beliefs.

NEXT STEPS

The first step is to have clients identify their motivators in the four quadrants: external negative, external positive, internal negative, and internal positive. The first worksheet **The Forces That Motivate** should be given to clients as homework, in session, or you can even do this as part of your intake packet for all of your clients, as this is critical information to know in regards to all of your clients. All five of the lines do not have to be completed, but knowing one or two in each quadrant is very valuable and helpful. Be aware that some motivators may be both internal and external, based upon how your client sees it. For example, clients may identify fear as both an external and internal negative motivator. In these cases, the internal versus external fears should be examined and clarified in session. The more concrete, the better.

Once you have the information in all four quadrants, you will ask your client to rank order them; use the second worksheet **The Forces That Motivate - Ranked** for this. The first motivator listed in each quadrant on the rank order worksheet is the one with the greatest influence, and it may also have the most significant history associated with it.

This activity involves recognizing the things in your life that motivate your thoughts and behaviors. There are four different quadrants below for you to identify your external negative, external positive, internal negative, and internal positive motivators. External motivators are those things in your life that are outside of yourself. For example, this may include times in which someone does something that motivates you to behave or think in a certain way.

An internal motivator is something inside of yourself, such as the hope for a better future or better relationships, which motivates you to engage in various behaviors and causes you to think a certain way. Motivators can be negative and/or positive based upon the person, his/her perspective, and the situation.

THE FORCES THAT MOTIVATE

Below is a list of internal and external motivators to help you identify your positive and negative internal and external motivators. Ask yourself, *"What motivates me?"* and put it in the appropriate quadrant on the next page. You can use an item from the lists below, or add your own.

INTERNAL MOTIVATORS	EXTERNAL MOTIVATORS
1. Enjoyment	1. Get good grades
2. Happiness	2. Avoid getting in trouble at home, work, or school
3. Sadness	3. Looking good to others
4. Avoid fear	4. Fear
5. Lack of trust in yourself	5. Avoid violence
6. Insecurity	6. Avoid ridicule
7. Doubt	7. Loose/earn respect
8. Loneliness	8. Encouragement
9. Determination	9. Kindness
10. Love	10. Someone is patient with you
11. Hope	11. Win awards
12. Desire	12. Get recognized
13. Self-satisfaction	13. Earn money
14. Meeting and beating a challenge	14. Sex
15. Excitement	15. Empathy – feel like someone understands you
16. Having fun	16. Feel appreciated
17. Compassion	17. Losing weight
18. Relieve stress	18. Prestige and status
19. Sense of accomplishment	19. Promotion at work
20. Feeling intelligent	20. Graduate with a degree
21. Pride	21. Avoid punishment
22. Curiosity	22. Appearing attractive
23. Anger	23. Being seen as smart
24. Rage	24. Fear of failure
25. Passion	25. Feel accepted

	NEGATIVE	POSITIVE
EXTERNAL		
INTERNAL		

THE FORCES THAT MOTIVATE-RANKED

Not all motivators have the same degree of influence. On this page, order your motivators in each of the four quadrants based upon how strongly they impact you. For example, if fear is a greater internal negative motivator than self-doubt, you would rank fear as #1 and self-doubt as #2 in the lower left quadrant. There are no right or wrong answers.

EXTERNAL	1. _____ 2. _____ 3. _____ 4. _____ 5. _____	1. _____ 2. _____ 3. _____ 4. _____ 5. _____
INTERNAL	1. _____ 2. _____ 3. _____ 4. _____ 5. _____	1. _____ 2. _____ 3. _____ 4. _____ 5. _____
	NEGATIVE	**POSITIVE**

THE INTRINSIC 4 AND THE VENEER OF PERFECTIONISM

The veneer of perfectionism is strong in individuals along the narcissistic spectrum. This veneer refers to an outer shell maintained by these individuals that nothing bothers them, that they have all the answers, and that if everyone would just do what they know to be right, everything would work out perfectly. To get a client along the narcissistic spectrum to work with you, you must first get underneath this veneer of perfectionism. You have to get behind the curtain. However, in order to do so, you have to first recognize critical factors that keep the veneer of perfectionism in place.

The intrinsic 4 are critical factors that you need to learn about and address in order to change maladaptive patterns in clients along the narcissistic spectrum. The intrinsic 4 are displayed below:

- **COMPETENCE**
- **AUTONOMY**
- **RELATEDNESS**
- **PURPOSE**

These four factors are derived from Self-Determination Theory (Deci & Ryan, 1985, 2000), which is an approach to motivation and personality that focuses on personal growth and getting intrinsic psychological needs met. These 4 factors are what keep the veneer of perfectionism in place, but we can utilize the 4 factors to get underneath it and begin to lessen the need to appear perfect and lessen the maladaptive behaviors and beliefs that go along with it. It is important to be aware that the intrinsic 4 are not focused on adaptive or maladaptive behaviors and beliefs; rather, they relate to what drives an individual's behavior to achieve his or her goal. In the case of individuals along the narcissistic spectrum, it is to appear as though they have no problems, have all the answers, are to never be questioned, and are above all others.

Before we apply the concept of the intrinsic 4, we need to define each according to Self-Determination Theory:

COMPETENCE	The need to be effective in dealing with the environment.
AUTONOMY	The need to be in control, be impactful, and have the freedom to choose how and when to do something. *This does not mean being independent.*
RELATEDNESS	The desire to have a close, affectionate relationship with others; belongingness.
PURPOSE	A drive to achieve satisfaction through goal attainment.

For the individual along the narcissistic spectrum, *competence* refers to the need to look effective and be perceived as perfect. This need is directly related to the veneer of perfectionism in that all of the individual's maladaptive behaviors and beliefs are directly associated with maintaining the perception that he or she has no flaws and possesses the knowledge and skills to masterfully complete anything. For individuals along the narcissistic spectrum, *autonomy* refers to the need to be in complete control of themselves, to be important and influential, and to have no constraints on their views and choices. The veneer of perfectionism is reinforced by the maladaptive behaviors and beliefs that demonstrate to others that they are not tethered to anyone, that people often seek them out for information and advice, and that they ultimately decide whether to provide such information and advice.

The intrinsic component of *relatedness* refers to the human drive to feel close and connected to others. This is a very contradictory drive for individuals along the narcissistic spectrum, as they desire to see themselves as an island, out there alone and not needing anyone else, but the reality is that they intensely need others for admiration, approval, and to achieve their needed sense of intellectual and/or physical superiority. You can specifically address the origins of this intrinsic need using the Doing It Differently worksheet. *Purpose* refers to the motivational need to achieve a sense of fulfillment. This drive also manifests in a contradictory manner for individuals along the narcissistic spectrum, as they set very low goals for themselves that are easily achieved in order to gain the sense of satisfaction and purpose that maintains their narcissism.

NEXT STEPS

Use the next worksheet, **The Intrinsic 4 of Goal Achievement**, to identify the intrinsic 4 in your client along the narcissistic spectrum. Each question is designed to elicit a response that will provide you, the mental health provider, with the insight needed to move forward to get underneath the veneer of perfectionism. Once you have the information you need, you will utilize it to make a greater and safer connection to your client. Remember, clients along the narcissistic spectrum are often fearful about the world around them and connecting to others, so a slow and cautious pace is critical for them to let down their guard (veneer of perfectionism) so you can help them change maladaptive behaviors and beliefs into adaptive ones.

THE INTRINSIC 4 OF GOAL ACHIEVEMENT

There are 4 factors that motivate us to achieve our goals: competence, autonomy, relatedness, and purpose. When we clearly identify what makes up these goals, we are better able to move toward them. Answer each question below without holding back or editing your thoughts and responses. Each question pertains to how you see yourself and under what circumstances others see you in the way you want them to.

You may not care how others see you, and that is fine. However, it is important to try and answer these questions, given that some goals are more easily achieved with the help of others. Just say whatever comes to your mind. There are no right or wrong answers.

I feel competent and skilled when: _____

_____

_____

People perceive me as competent when: _____

_____

_____

I feel influential and impactful when: _____

_____   _____

_____

People perceive me as influential and impactful when: _____

_____

_____

I feel ready to connect with others when: _____

_____

_____

People perceive me as wanting to connect with them when: _____

_____

_____

I feel a sense of purpose when: _____

_____

_____

People perceive me as being satisfied with my goals when: _____

_____

_____

NARCISSISTIC REACTIONS: FROM STRESS TO RAGE

The hardest part about the successful treatment of individuals along the narcissistic spectrum is identifying and managing the symptoms associated with the expression of narcissistic rage. Narcissistic rage is well known to disrupt the course of treatment and tends to cause significant issues in clients' lives and that of those around them. The most common prelude to a narcissistic rage response is the incurring of a narcissistic wound. A narcissistic wound is any psychological experience that clients have that causes them to feel that their hidden "true self" has been exposed, which subsequently causes them to feel vulnerable.

The two types of narcissistic rage are illustrated below, along with three critical identifiers:

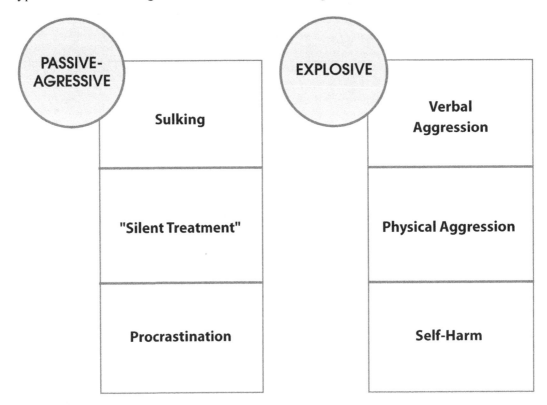

When most individuals hear the word "rage," they tend to associate it with the explosive type. This type of rage is associated with the outward expression of extreme anger, which manifests as yelling, throwing things, hitting things, or even becoming physically aggressive with others. In some cases, individuals will also harm themselves when responding in an explosive narcissistic rage.

However, there is also a second type of narcissistic rage, which is the "passive-aggressive" type. In this case, individuals along the narcissistic spectrum may brood or mope about, not speak to others to let them know they are hurt, or purposely procrastinate to cause frustration in the individual who caused the narcissistic wound.

It is important to recognize that these rage types exist on a continuum (shown below), ranging from individuals who are prone to both types of rage responses (high explosive, high passive-aggressive) to those who are prone to neither (low explosive, low passive-aggressive). The manner in which the rage is expressed is influenced by core factors specific to the individual; to learn more about core and surface structure issues associated with NPD, see the chapter and accompanying worksheet titled Identifying Surface and Core Structures of Narcissistic Personality Disorder.

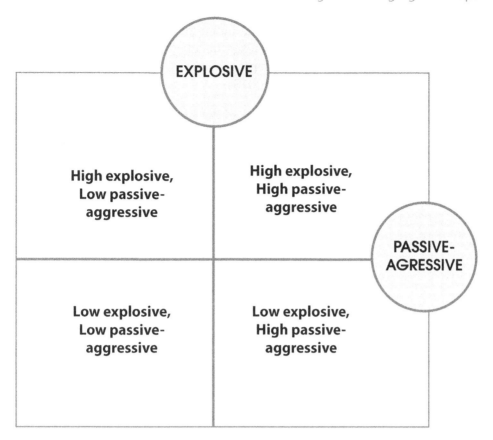

It is important for therapists to have a clear picture of where the clients are along the narcissistic rage response continuum and in which direction they are likely to go after incurring a narcissistic wound. Clients' responses tend to reveal a lot about how they will react as they move through the treatment process. Narcissistic wounds are part of the treatment process, as no treatment trajectory goes perfectly, smoothly, or without some degree of dissonance. Therefore, when working with clients along the narcissistic spectrum, knowing what to be "on the lookout for" when they experience a stressful event that may cause a narcissistic wound is an invaluable part of the treatment process.

NEXT STEPS

The **Stress Reaction** worksheet provided next will help you and/or your client recognize the progression of his or her narcissistic rage response. In identifying its course, you can implement coping mechanisms, treatment interventions, or alternative thoughts or behaviors to attenuate the narcissistic rage. Provide your client with the worksheet, and examine the progression from stress to where he or she is along the continuum ranging from explosive rage to passive-aggressive rage. You can do this exercise in an individual session, as homework, or in a group setting.

The first part of the exercise asks clients to identify the source of the stressor (e.g., environmental, emotional, or a thought or image in their head, such as being discarded or mistreated). There can be more than one source of stress, so this is not an "either/or" situation. For example, stress can originate from an environmental cause and an ensuing thought that your client has in response to that environmental stressor. After identifying the source(s) of stress, clients will then identify how they interpret the stressful situation. The worksheet provides clients with some options to help with their interpretation, as well as a space to include their own ideas. Next, possible initial reactions are listed from which clients can choose, and a space is provided to include thoughts of their own.

The last section asks clients to identify where on the continuum they fall that best represents how they behave following the initial stress reaction. The closer that clients are to the explosive type of narcissistic rage, the more they may benefit from anger management, and you will want to rule out Intermittent Explosive Disorder in the *DSM-5* (APA, 2013).

To help clients counteract their rage episodes, take a look at the **Lengthening the Fuse to Prevent Explosions** worksheet provided in this workbook. The closer that clients are to the passive-aggressive type of narcissistic rage, the more they may benefit from assertiveness training, and you may want to use the **Assertiveness over Aggression** worksheet in this workbook.

Remember, it can take less than one second for the stressful situation to escalate into a narcissistic rage response. Slowing this process down and providing valuable insight is critical for your client to derail this process and learn more functional response patterns.

STRESS REACTION

This worksheet is going to help you identify your source(s) of stress, as well as your reaction to these stressors. Doing so will help you have greater insight, power, and control over it. Be as descriptive as you can when identifying the source of your stress. There can be more than one source of stress, so this is not an "either/or" situation.

For example, stress can originate from an environmental cause and from any subsequent thoughts you have in response to that environmental stressor. The chart below is designed to help you identify your environmental, emotional, or thought/image stressors. It is okay to list your own stressors if they are not listed below.

ENVIRONMENTAL	EMOTIONAL	THOUGHT/IMAGE
• Increase in workload	• Depression	• They don't respect me
• Divorce	• Anxiety	• They think I am stupid
• Financial obligations	• Fear	• They don't listen to me
• Moving to a new place or job	• Sadness	• I can see myself as homeless
• Passed over for a promotion	• Anger	• I picture everyone laughing at me

• **Environmental:** _____

_____

_____

• **Emotional:** _____

_____

_____

_____

• **Thought/Image:** _____

_____

_____

_____

How did you interpret the source of stress? Mark (√) all that apply:

- ☐ Challenged my confidence
- ☐ Reduced/removed my control
- ☐ Offended me

- ☐ Made me look bad
- ☐ Hurt my feelings
- ☐ Feel exposed/unmasked

- ☐ Felt like I was going to be hurt
- ☐ Made me feel isolated/alone
- ☐ Made me feel small

Other (describe your interpretation):

_____

_____

What is/was your initial reaction(s)? Mark (√) all that apply:

- ☐ Denial
- ☐ Anxious
- ☐ Irritated

- ☐ Restless
- ☐ Sad
- ☐ Guilty

- ☐ Overwhelmed
- ☐ Helpless
- ☐ Hopeless

- ☐ Apathy
- ☐ Unappreciated
- ☐ Rage

Other (describe your interpretation):

_____

_____

Using the following scales to identify how much Type A and Type B are like you. A chart describing both types of responses is on the next page to help you. Return this to your mental health provider when you are done.

TYPE A
Sulk/mope
Give others the "silent treatment"
Procrastinate

```
0          1          2          3          4          5
```
**Not at all
like me**   **Very much
                                                   like me**

- -

TYPE B
Become verbally aggressive
Become physically aggressive
Harm myself

```
0          1          2          3          4          5
```
**Not at all
like me**   **Very much
                                                   like me**

BUILDING AND BREAKING INTERPERSONAL CONNECTIONS

Connecting to others is a basic human need, and even individuals along the narcissistic spectrum are not immune from this need. In fact, they are often driven by an intense urge to connect to others in order to support and validate their sense of narcissism. Gaining a sense of understanding regarding the value that clients put on others is critical to lessen their maladaptive narcissistic behaviors and beliefs.

Most individuals along the narcissistic spectrum place seemingly very little value in others and will often rate those closest to them as having very little impact. However, the reality is that clients likely value interpersonal connections more than they are willing to admit. Once you have gotten underneath the veneer of perfectionism (see worksheet on The Intrinsic 4 and the Veneer of Perfectionism activity in this workbook), you can assess the value that clients place on those within their interpersonal circle. This is a frightening activity for many individuals along this spectrum, as closeness implies the ability to be hurt, abandoned, and rendered unimportant.

Before helping clients build or break interpersonal connections, ask them this seemingly simple question:

HOW IMPORTANT ARE THE PEOPLE IN YOUR LIFE?

The answer to this question will tell you if your client along the narcissistic spectrum is ready to build or break any interpersonal connections because before you can build it or break it, you have to see it as impactful and valuable. You can move forward if your client answers this question with any of the following: "a lot," "some," "a little," or even "I don't know." If clients answer "none," or any synonym thereof, this is an indicator you are not under the veneer of perfectionism and that they are not ready to acknowledge their vulnerability to others within their interpersonal circle. At this point in treatment, you need to go back to relationship building and gaining trust.

When clients do respond with a value of importance (i.e., a lot, some, or a little) or an uncertain response (i.e., I don't know), they are ready to assess and evaluate those interpersonal connections. In particular, they are now ready to build on the relationships in which they feel safe and break the ones that promote maladaptive behaviors and beliefs characteristic of narcissism. You will then ask clients to assess the degree of importance that they give to that identified person in their life.

To determine the degree of importance that clients place on the relationships they have with others, you will use the Gauge of Importance. The gauge is to be used as a graphical means to identify that level of importance, as shown below and in the worksheet that follows:

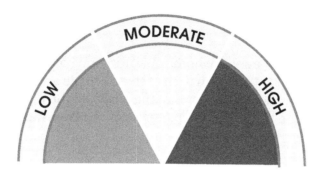

Clients are instructed to gauge the level of importance that they place on others as Low, Moderate, or High. The value placed on these identified individuals will help clients recognize how important others are, or are not, to them and provide a graphical representation of that. For each of the individuals whom clients list, they will be asked to think about the relationship to determine if they want to build it or break it. Building it implies learning relationship management skills (see Strengthening Social Potency worksheet) and/or assertiveness training (see Assertiveness over Aggression worksheet).

When breaking or ending relationships, many individuals along the narcissistic spectrum do so with all of the dramatic and erratic flare they can muster. They decimate the relationship with violence, acting out, blaming, and other maladaptive behaviors. In contrast, breaking the relationship in a therapeutic manner entails opening the door to learning adaptive behaviors to dissolve a relationship.

NEXT STEPS

Provide clients with the **Gauge of Importance** worksheet and ask them to list each person in their life who they feel has some degree of value or impact, and identify that person's value. Ask clients to consider the interactions they have with each of these people and how much value they place on the relationship, that person's opinion, and the impact that this person has on them, either directly or indirectly. Direct impact could be from someone like a parent, significant other, or boss, and indirect impact could be from someone they admire or a friend of a friend. Clients will then mark the level of importance on the meter below as Low, Moderate, or High.

Once the first part has been completed, provide clients with the **Build It or Break It?** worksheet, and ask them to write down the name of one of the individuals whom they listed on the previous page. Then, ask them to describe why they should build it or break it, as well as what they can do to enhance the relationship or end it in the most beneficial manner.

GAUGE OF IMPORTANCE

Use the spaces below to list those people whom you value who have some degree of impact on you. Consider the interactions that you have with each of these people and how much value you place on the relationship, their opinion, and the impact that they have on the relationship, either directly or indirectly. Mark the level of importance on the meter below as: **Low, Moderate, or High.**

_____

_____

_____

_____

_____

BUILD IT OR BREAK IT?

Think about the relationship that you have with each of the individuals you listed on the **Gauge of Importance** worksheet, and determine if you want to build the relationship or break it (end it).

Write the name of one of the individuals whom you listed on the previous page on the line below, describe why you would want to build the relationship or break it, and describe what you can do to enhance the relationship or end it in the most beneficial manner.

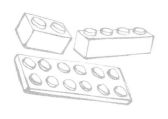

_____

Build It or Break It
(write name above)

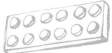

Why: _____

_____

_____

What I can do: _____

_____

_____

_____

Digging Deeper into Motivations and Lessening Symptomatology

ENHANCING PERSONAL EMPOWERMENT TO LESSEN MALADAPTIVE NARCISSISTIC BEHAVIORS

Power and the desire to achieve it is a core issue for many individuals along the narcissistic spectrum. For such individuals, power as a core structure component is related to "fantasies of unlimited success, power, brilliance, beauty, or ideal love" (APA, 2013, p. 669). Individuals along the narcissistic spectrum are fixated on thoughts about admiration and privilege while comparing themselves to famous others who have significant influence. The reality is that most individuals along the narcissistic spectrum achieve very little because they do not take risks to achieve their dreams, which directly feeds their narcissistic maladaptive behaviors and beliefs.

There are times when you can clearly see the defenses that your clients put in place to protect this core structure and the value they place on power. For example, this becomes evident in your clients' reactions when they are in challenging situations, their goals are not achieved, and others make note of a failure or are perceived to stand in their way. The reaction typically involves physical or verbal attacks, passive-aggressive behavior, or intense blaming of others for their failure. To lessen these maladaptive behaviors, we have to examine and treat the underlying core structure, which typically entails fear, shame, guilt, doubt, and/or inferiority (see worksheet titled Identifying Surface and Core Structures of Narcissistic Personality Disorder to help pinpoint core structure and surface structure behaviors).

An effective way to lessen narcissistic maladaptive behaviors associated with clients' core need for power is to explore and enhance their genuine personal empowerment. By meeting this core need in a more adaptive manner, clients along the narcissistic spectrum are able to gain intrinsic benefit, incur greater rewards and satisfaction with themselves, and not harm themselves or others.

It is important to note that you will not exacerbate your clients' narcissism by enhancing their sense of personal empowerment. While narcissism is most often viewed in a negative light, there are healthy components to narcissism as well (e.g., general well-being, self-assurance, self-assertion, satisfaction with oneself that motivates fantasies of love, achievement, and ambition). However, it is the maladaptive behaviors and beliefs that tend to garner the spotlight and cause problems in these clients' lives and in the lives of those around them.

The following activity will pinpoint the 5 areas on which to focus in treatment in order to enhance personal empowerment:

AWARENESS	VALUES	SKILLS	INFORMATION	GOALS

Awareness entails gaining an understanding that one's intent influences behavior, which determines the consequence. This is a critical first step in recognizing the difference between adaptive and maladaptive patterns, including which patterns are associated with a greater probability of positive outcomes. The *Values* factor involves exploring what is important and motivating to your clients, as well as how they would be affected by any potential losses in these areas. The *Skills* factor explores the areas in which your client does well, does poorly, and could improve upon. It also examines your clients' ability to ask for help when needed. *Information* explores how clients along the narcissistic spectrum treat incoming data, knowledge, and stimuli that they encounter and want to disseminate to the world. The final factor that can enhance personal empowerment is *Goals*. This factor includes breaking down goals in an operationally defined manner by describing what goals are attainable versus challenging, as well as what clients hope to achieve.

NEXT STEPS

Provide your clients with **The 5 Factors to Enhance Personal Empowerment** worksheet, and ask them to fill it out as best they can. You will notice that the instructions are designed to lessen narcissistic resistance and encourage honest and insight-oriented responses. Some of the questions may frustrate your clients, but it is important that you give them the freedom to express that frustration on the worksheet.

Once they have completed the worksheet, go through it with your clients and look for themes that indicate core structural concerns (e.g., fear, shame, guilt, doubt, and/or inferiority), as well as how they see the world. Many individuals along the narcissistic spectrum see the world as "out to get me" and "prove me wrong." By adding clarity to these critical aspects, you are helping increase your clients' insight and build appropriate assertiveness skills when they are in a challenging situation.

This is a good exercise to complete multiple times throughout the therapy process in order to illustrate gains made by your clients, which reinforces their working with you to lessen surface structure maladaptive behaviors and to build a more adaptive core structure.

THE 5 FACTORS TO ENHANCE PERSONAL EMPOWERMENT

This worksheet will help you explore the five factors that will build a sense of power and success. The five factors include: **Awareness, Values, Skills, Information, and Goals**. With this knowledge, you and your therapist can help design pathways to success and achievement. You are the critical component in this activity, and it requires that you answer each question to the best of your ability and as honestly and completely as you can.

AWARENESS

When you are in challenging situations, what is your intent (put an X over all those that apply)**?**

Win at all Costs	Destroy my opponent	Be noticed	Be happy with myself	Make self and other proud

What is your "go to" behavior in situations that are challenging to you?

_____

_____

In challenging situations, do you tend to react (put an X over which one is more like you)**:**

QUICKLY	CAUTIOUSLY

How much do you believe in the following statements on a scale from 1 to 10 (1 = do not believe at all; 10 = completely believe)?

Positive behavior increases the probability of positive outcomes

1	2	3	4	5	6	7	8	9	10

Negative behavior increases the probability of negative outcomes

1	2	3	4	5	6	7	8	9	10

VALUES

What do you value? _____

_____

_____

What is of importance to you? _____

_____

_____

What would you miss if it (something/someone of value to you) were not there?

_____

_____

What motivates you? _____

_____

_____

SKILLS

What do you do well? _____

_____

_____

What do you do poorly? _____

_____

_____

What could you do better? _____

_____

_____

Who could you ask for help? _____

_____

_____

INFORMATION

What information do you need to change how you see the world?

_____

_____

What information do you want to give to the world? _____

_____

_____

What information has value to you (personal, monetary, social, etc.)**?**

_____

_____

What information keeps you stuck (i.e., is so intense that it is hard to not think about)**?**

_____

_____

What information helps you get what you want? _____

_____

_____

GOALS

How will you know your goal(s) have been achieved? _____

_____

_____

What are your short-term and long-term goals?

Short-term goals: _____

_____

_____

Long-term goals: _____

_____

_____

What are your dream goals? _____

_____

_____

What are difficult or challenging goals you want to achieve? _____

_____

_____

What do you want? _____

_____

_____

ASSERTIVENESS OVER AGGRESSION

Individuals along the narcissistic spectrum are treatment rejecting. They do not see a use for mental health treatment in most cases. However, if you are working with someone along this spectrum, something has occurred, and, regretfully, aggression is usually part of the impetus to attend treatment. Although mental health providers are never surprised by the surface structure behavior of narcissistic aggression and rage (see the worksheet on **Narcissistic Reactions: From Stress to Rage** for further information on identifying the rage type your client exhibits), we have to get to the core structure that is driving the aggression in order to attenuate it, and your client must be willing to explore it with you. In this respect, two sets of studies by Bushman and Baumeister (1998) help shed light on the relationship between narcissism and aggressive responses.

In these two studies, they provided participants an opportunity to act aggressively toward an innocent third party, toward someone who had insulted them, or toward someone who had praised them. Results showed that individuals high in narcissism exhibited the most aggressive responses, particularly toward individuals who had given them an insulting, negative evaluation. However, when individuals high on narcissism received praise, they were less likely to exhibit an aggressive response. These studies illustrate what many mental health providers observe in clients along the narcissistic spectrum: when these individuals incur a narcissistic wound, they attack the person who caused the wound in an aggressive manner.

When clients along the narcissistic spectrum have an aggressive reaction, do you know where it came from, what aspect of their core structure was triggered, or how they felt attacked? Did your client feel fear, shame, guilt, doubt, or inferior to someone else? It is critical to be able to answer these questions if you are going to change the trajectory of the response from aggressive to assertive.

NEXT STEPS

First complete the **Assertiveness over Aggression Therapist Form** to help you determine the core structure of the aggression. Doing this will help you gain insight into what is driving the narcissistic aggressive behavior, who was impacted, and the value placed on those who were impacted. Knowing this information can help you tap into your client's motivation to do things differently.

If you are in this section of the workbook, you are likely working with someone who recognizes the need to change and is willing to put some trust in you and the process. Sometimes you will need to remind your clients that they are more likely to get a positive outcome when behaving assertively over aggressively. Provide them with multiple examples to make this clear. One example is provided below:

Aggressive: Tony began yelling at his daughter for coming home late as soon as she walked through the door. As he was yelling at her, she rolled her eyes and stomped upstairs. Tony continued to yell at her, eventually grabbed her cell phone, and smashed it with a hammer to "teach her a lesson."

Assertive: Tony's daughter came home late. When she walked through the door, he asked her to come into the living room and sit down. In a calm and concerned tone, he explained to her that when she is late, he is worried that she is hurt, and he starts to get anxious that someone so special to him could be hurt and that he would not be there to help her. His daughter apologized for being late and went up to her room.

You can process these two scenarios with your client. Which is most effective and beneficial? Hopefully, your client recognizes that Tony not only dealt with the situation in the second scenario in a more beneficial manner and had a greater likelihood of achieving his goal (i.e., his daughter coming home on time), but he also did something more: he strengthened his relationship with his daughter. This last point can sometimes be difficult for individuals along the narcissistic spectrum to grasp, as they tend to want immediate results, compliance, and gratification. However, relationships do not always work that way.

Next, provide clients with the **Assertiveness over Aggression** worksheet. This worksheet will take them through the incident that ignited the aggressive response, the core structural components that were triggered, their ensuing response, its consequences, the willingness to recognize alternatives, what they could have done differently, the consequences of alternative behavior, and three critical assertiveness skills (communication, win-win, and avoidance) to do things differently next time. Use future sessions to focus on one or all three of the assertiveness skills, and help your clients infuse them into their response pattern. Skill building takes time and effort, and assertiveness skills certainly fall into that category.

ASSERTIVENESS OVER AGGRESSION

Describe the aggressive behavior: _____

_____

_____

What triggered the aggression? _____

_____

_____

What aspect of your client's core was triggered (put an X over all that apply)?

(FEAR)   (SHAME)   (GUILT)   (DOUBT)   (INFERIORITY)

Write the name and relationship of those who have been impacted by the aggressive response (spouse, child, friends, etc.):

Of those impacted, whom do you perceive as having the greatest value in the eyes of your client?

_____

_____

ASSERTIVENESS OVER AGGRESSION

Complete the exercise below to help you examine situations where you have had an aggressive response (or people to whom you have had an aggressive response), and explore the assertiveness options you have that increase your control in situations where you are likely to lose your temper or have negative consequences. Answer each question as honestly and completely as you can. There are no wrong answers.

Remember a situation that drove you to behave in an aggressive manner.

Rate how you feel currently when you think about this situation on a scale from 1 to 10 (1 = state of complete calm; 10 = rage)**:**

1	2	3	4	5	6	7	8	9	10

Describe what caused the situation: _____

_____

_____

Put an X over any of the following feelings you felt in this situation aside from anger:

FEAR   SHAME   GUILT   DOUBT   INFERIORITY

Describe what you did in this situation: _____

_____

_____

Describe the conclusion of the situation: _____

_____

_____

Describe the impact that this conclusion had on you and your life:

_____

_____

Do you wish you had done something differently (put an X over your answer)?

YES	NO

If yes, describe what you wish you had done differently: _____

_____

_____

If no, describe what worked for you in this situation: _____

_____

_____

If you were in this situation again, do you think you would be better off if you maintained control of your aggression (put an X over your answer)?

YES	NO

Do you think it is important to communicate your expectations, needs, and wants to others effectively (put an X over your answer)?

YES	NO

If yes, try this exercise:

HOW TO COMMUNICATE YOUR EXPECTATIONS, NEEDS, AND WANTS EFFECTIVELY
Make an assertive request or statement using an "I" statement. For example: "I need you to do this today or it will be late" or "I get worried you are not hearing me when you do not do what I asked."

When your wants or needs are in conflict, can you look for a win-win situation (put an X over your answer)?

YES	NO

If yes, try this exercise:

THE WIN-WIN SITUATION
• Make it about the relationship and not the person – "separate the person from the problem."
• Generate a variety of options that offer gains to both parties before deciding what to do.
• Aim for the result to be based on an objective standard, not just for you.

Can you avoid other people who are aggressive, abusive, and critical (put an X over your answer)?

YES	NO

If yes, try this exercise:

ASSERTIVE AVOIDANCE
Recognize and avoid those with whom you tend to have an aggressive, abusive, and critical relationship. Leaving a situation where you have a high likelihood of being aggressive is a powerful and assertive decision. Why is it powerful? Because you made the choice to exit the situation, and you controlled it by not allowing it to set you off on an aggressive response path.

LENGTHENING THE FUSE TO PREVENT EXPLOSIONS

Many individuals along the narcissistic spectrum are short-term hedonists, a term coined by Albert Ellis (Bernard & Ellis, 2011). Short-term hedonists are those who focus on the immediate or short-term payoffs that provide the greatest amount of pleasure. Pleasure for those along the narcissistic spectrum includes anything that reinforces their view of the world and justifies their behavior to get their needs met. The problem with this approach is that it causes significant collateral damage to those around them. At home, people try to adjust their schedules to avoid this person, say only unimportant and insignificant things to keep this individual calm and happy, and often hide critical details about their lives so they do not cause a behavioral explosion. At work, co-workers avoid, exclude, kowtow (act in an excessively subservient manner), and, in some cases, engage in behaviors to get this person fired.

In both of these environments, individuals along the narcissistic spectrum are getting exactly what they feared: disingenuous and unauthentic behavior, thoughts, and reactions. This, in turn, further justifies their maladaptive views and lowers their frustration tolerance, which increases the probability of behavioral explosions or aggression (see worksheet titled **Assertiveness over Aggression** for more on acknowledging and managing aggression). Throughout the treatment process, lengthening the fuse to behavioral explosions will be revisited over and over again, as this issue is likely to continue to manifest but hopefully in ways that are less explosive and produce less collateral damage. **The Lengthening of the Fuse** exercise is designed to identify common areas that reduce the fuse and that increase the probability of a behavioral explosion, followed by steps to counteract it.

NEXT STEPS

Provide your clients with **The Lengthening of the Fuse** worksheet, and ask them to review it and answer the initial three questions. Exploring the answers to these three questions can take multiple therapy sessions, but it is an important place to begin. Clients' willingness to even examine the 7 fuse reducers is a terrific sign of their motivation to control this aspect of themselves and overcome it. You should recognize their willingness and praise them for it. It is undoubtedly difficult for your client.

Once you feel that you have explored the 7 fuse reducers, give your client **The 12 Fuse Enhancers** activity. This activity entails giving your clients the opportunity to explore techniques to lessen the probability of a behavioral explosion, help them sustain control, and increase the benefits gained from various encounters. An explanation of each coping strategy is provided below, after which your client will be asked to rank order all 12 strategies from "most likely to try" to "will never try." Even if clients choose only one strategy, that is still a move in the right direction and tells you that they are open to learning new coping strategies to gain control over their behavior.

Be sure to have them implement the coping strategies on multiple occasions to help them learn the skills that they need to better control their behavioral explosions.

THE LENGTHENING OF THE FUSE

The seven most common components that lead to a behavioral explosion are listed below. Take a moment to examine each of these and ask yourself these 3 questions:

1. How common are behavioral explosions in my life?
2. How do behavioral explosions impact me?
3. What have I done when I have exploded in the past?

THE 7 FUSE REDUCERS

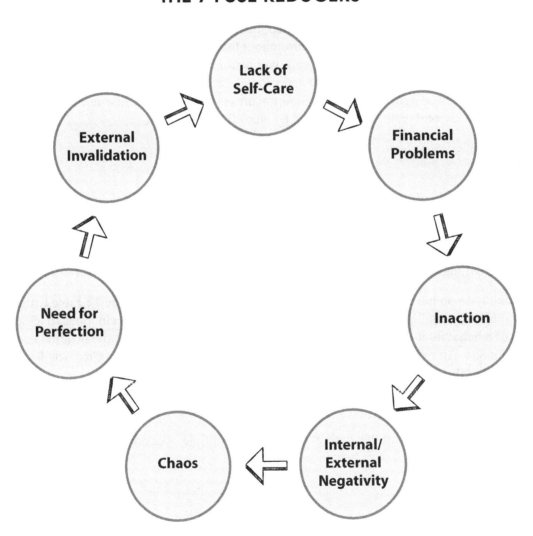

Take some time and discuss these with your therapist before moving on to the 12 fuse enhancers.

THE 12 FUSE ENHANCERS

The 12 fuse enhancers are the mechanisms to help you maintain control and increase the probability of maximizing the benefit from various situations you may encounter. An explanation of each strategy is provided below, followed by a form to allow you to rank each strategy from "most likely to try" to "will never try."

IT'S YOUR CHOICE TO REACT	BE A LONG-TERM HEDONIST	SET ACHIEVABLE GOALS EACH DAY
PRACTICE DECISION-MAKING	THINK OUTSIDE YOUR BOX	REFRAME STRESSFUL SITUATIONS
PROVIDE CONTEXT	HEALTHY DISTRACTIONS	ACT "AS IF"
EXPOSURE	UNCONDITIONAL SELF-ACCEPTANCE	MINDFULNESS

It's Your Choice to React entails empowering yourself with choice. When we allow our fuses to burn quickly, we lose time to consider the alternatives to and consequences of our behavior. When you are in a situation and you feel your fuse shortening (imagine a stick of dynamite and the fuse burning quickly), slow down and consider your responsibility in the situation, as well as the responsibility of others who are involved. Examine your goal in the situation, what the ideal outcome is, and what you need from the situation. By doing this, you empower yourself with choice because it's your choice to react or not.

Be a Long-Term Hedonist includes recognizing the long-term gains of your behavior and fighting the urge to be a short-term hedonist, which involves engaging in an immediate response to fulfill a short-term – and usually fleeting – want or perceived need. What are your long-term goals, and what can you do to achieve them? The long-term hedonist is usually happier, more satisfied, and succeeds more often.

Set Achievable Goals Each Day that you can achieve in one day, visualize your achievement, write it down, identify its purpose, commit to a strategy that works, focus on your daily goal, map out your plan of action, engage in behavior that moves you forward, and hold yourself accountable for what you can control and not for what you cannot control.

Practice Decision-Making entails making decisions that benefit you and possibly someone else. Decision-making is a skill like roller skating: the more you do it, the better you get. The decision-making process typically has seven steps: (1) identify the purpose of the decision, (2) gather relevant information, (3) brainstorm and analyze your different choices, (4) evaluate your alternatives, (5) select the best alternative, (6) execute your decision, and (7) evaluate the results. Decision-making can take seconds or hours, depending upon the choice you have to make, which means that patience with yourself and sometimes others is another component of practicing decision-making.

Think Outside Your Box involves examining your usual choices and responses in situations where you would typically explode, and then challenging yourself to devise alternative behavioral patterns to meet your goals. To help think outside your box, you may want to brainstorm ideas with your therapist to get an impartial analysis of alternative options you have not previously considered.

Reframe Stressful Situations entails examining a stressful situation and recognizing your tendency to focus on the negatives of not getting what you want while ignoring the positives. To reframe your situation, you must first detach yourself from the stress to better assess the situation because agitation colors our view. Next, go over the situation in your mind, and put your emotions to the side, but allow your frustration to float out of it. If you start to get frustrated, breathe, and let it go. Then, pay attention to any "popping thoughts" you may have. These are thoughts that pop into your mind when you get agitated or frustrated. Perhaps these thoughts are about your mistreatment, what is unfair, etc. Next, assess what evidence is available to support your "popping thoughts" in the situation, look for contrary evidence, and use this evidence to create fair and balanced thoughts. This is an exercise to do over and over again, and as you do it more, you will see that it becomes automatic and more helpful.

Provide Context is when you evaluate a situation, look beyond your part, and examine the overall circumstances, including how it impacts you and those around you. It is important to recognize the positives and negatives for each person and group involved in the situation. This gives you a global view, as opposed to a narrow view, which tends to be a common precursor to behavioral explosions.

Healthy Distractions can be anything that helps you grow and develop while reducing the probability of a behavioral explosion. These distractions can include watching a funny or inspiring movie or TV show, exercising, reading an inspiring book or story, playing with a dog or cat, allowing yourself to sit and do nothing, painting, writing, drinking water (yes, water helps to lessen agitation, whereas dehydration increases it), or reminding yourself that "this will pass." The list can go on and on. Try to discover some distractions that fit for you.

Act "As If" is a psychological technique originally devised by Austrian psychotherapist Alfred Adler. In the case of lessening behavioral explosions, it entails acting as if you are in a particular state of calm and that no one can upset you. You act "as if" you are imperturbable, which means that you are even-tempered and cannot become upset or excitable. You act as if you are as "cool as a cucumber." This technique has also been labeled, "fake it till you make it."

Exposure entails forcing yourself to go into a situation in which you would normally be frustrated and likely to have a behavioral explosion. Start slowly, and increase the amount of time you expose yourself to the situation according to a preset plan. For example, start once a week or once a day, and then expand it to twice a week or twice a day. You will find that over time, you build a greater sense of control, and your frustration lessens.

Unconditional Self-Acceptance (USA) includes allowing yourself to accept the imperfections that we all have. It involves saying to yourself, "I accept myself because I am alive, and I am who I am," and meaning it. For some people, practicing self-acceptance is a lifelong journey, but those who make gains in this area are more impactful in their lives and the lives of those around them.

Mindfulness is the state of being conscious or aware of something. It is not synonymous with meditation. It involves enhancing focus, while calmly acknowledging and accepting your thoughts, feelings, and bodily sensations. To practice mindfulness, follow these four steps: (1) take a deep breath and relax; (2) focus on your breathing, start counting your breaths from 1 to 10, then start over, noticing the sound of your breathing and its warmth; (3) once your focus has narrowed, begin to widen it and notice sounds, sensations, and your thoughts; and (4) notice each thought or sensation without judging it as good or bad. If your mind starts to race, return your focus to your breathing, and then expand your awareness again. Practice this technique multiple times per day. It does not take long, but it is an amazing skill to develop.

Rank order the likelihood that you would try each of these 12 fuse enhancers on a scale from 1 to 10 (1 = most likely to try, 10 = will never try).

IT'S YOUR CHOICE TO REACT	BE A LONG-TERM HEDONIST	SET ACHIEVABLE GOALS EACH DAY
_____	_____	_____
PRACTICE DECISION-MAKING	THINK OUTSIDE YOUR BOX	REFRAME STRESSFUL SITUATIONS
_____	_____	_____
PROVIDE CONTEXT	HEALTHY DISTRACTIONS	ACT "AS IF"
_____	_____	_____
EXPOSURE	UNCONDITIONAL SELF-ACCEPTANCE	MINDFULNESS
_____	_____	_____

DOING IT DIFFERENTLY

Many clients are reluctant to change because they perceive the process as one that involves shedding who they are and becoming someone totally new. Imagine if you removed who you are, the good parts and the bad, and were molded into someone new because who you previously were was not good enough. This idea would frighten anyone, though it is even more disconcerting for those individuals along the narcissistic spectrum, as they are contending with their own mixture of fear, shame, guilt, doubt, and inferiority. With all of these factors against them – and also against you as their mental health provider – you must get them aligned with you in order to get them to change their usual course and learn to do things differently.

Individuals along the narcissistic spectrum have internal representations and roles that have been created and continually reinforced through maladaptive patterns that feed their core structural issues of fear, shame, guilt, doubt, and inferiority. The following activity gets to that core structure and finds more advantageous ways to get their needs met. These include utilizing more adaptive strategies to achieve their goals without having to psychologically destroy others who do not immediately see their perspective, which ultimately causes them harm.

There are five steps to helping clients along the narcissistic spectrum to do things differently:

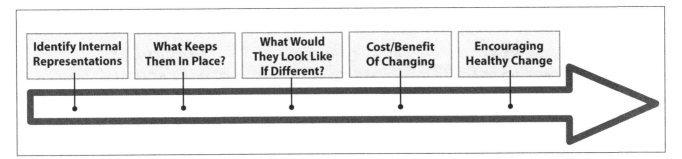

Internal representations (also known as internal working models) were initially proposed by John Bowlby (1988), and refer to the expectations, rules, or beliefs that individuals use to understand themselves, others, and their world. According to Bowlby, these internal working models are formed in childhood through the interactions that individuals have with attachment figures, particularly during infancy. These internal representations help to organize personality and influence future relationships by creating a template that shapes thoughts, feelings, and behaviors about oneself and others. When working to identify your client's internal representation to influence future therapeutic growth, you must know which internal representation is present. Many clients understand these internal representations best as if their life is a movie in which they are playing a role.

To dig deeper and change narcissistic symptomatology, we have to not only define the roles into which our clients fall, but we must also determine what keeps them in these roles, challenge them to do things differently, and enhance their self-evaluation skills. Typically, internal representations and roles are maintained because they reinforce your clients' views of the world and create a sense of safety in their routines, regardless if it is adaptive or maladaptive. Thus, it is not surprising that clients are initially reluctant to do things differently. Increasing insight into the purpose of your clients' roles is critical to assess how to challenge those roles and the motivators that keep them in place. Doing so will allow clients to evaluate and experience new opportunities that influence the direction of their lives in a more authentic and adaptive manner.

NEXT STEPS

Provide your client along the narcissistic spectrum with the **Doing It Differently** worksheet. You can give this as homework or complete it together in session. Think about what role into which you believe your client falls, and after your client completes the activity, go over it together to see if your conceptualization matches that of the client; this makes for great therapeutic process and discussion. The final step, which is not included as part of the activity, involves encouraging healthy change. Most mental health providers do this naturally, and, in this case, you want to be sure to identify what your client can do next that represents a healthy change and weave this into your therapeutic approach going forward.

DOING IT DIFFERENTLY

This exercise is designed to help you identify the roles into which you fall in your life, what motivates you to stay in those roles, how your world would be different if you changed certain aspects of those roles, and the perceived cost and benefit of changing.

If your life were a movie, what roles would you see yourself playing in your life? These roles are based upon the expectations, rules, or beliefs that you learned growing up.

Mark (√) any and all of the roles that you feel apply to you. The last box is provided in case you fall into a role that is not listed below.

☐ Mother	☐ Father	☐ Daughter	☐ Son
☐ Provider	☐ God	☐ Lover	☐ Parent
☐ Neglector	☐ Blamer	☐ Revealer	☐ Failure
☐ Hero	☐ Worker	☐ Friend	☐ Loner
☐ Husband	☐ Wife	☐ King	☐ Queen
☐ Scholar	☐ Warrior	☐ Joker	☐ Chameleon
☐ Prince	☐ Princess	☐ Scapegoat	☐ Abuser
☐ Other:			

Mark (√) any and all of the motivators that keep your roles in place. Some are listed below, and there is also space to include any of your own that are not listed here.

☐ Shows people how special I am	☐ Keeps others away
☐ Shows others how powerful I am	☐ Keeps me from getting too close
☐ Keeps others at a safe distance	☐ Provides me with control
☐ Gives responsibility to others	☐ Prevents me from being rejected
☐ Shows people how I really feel about them	☐ Keeps me safe
☐ Shows others that they cannot hurt me	☐ Prevents me from getting hurt
☐ Shows people my uniqueness	☐ Hides who I really am
☐ Other:	

By challenging those roles and motivators, you open yourself to new opportunities to influence the direction of your life and the people within it. Answer each of the sentence stems below with how your world would be different if you were:

More Honest: _____

_____

More Dependable: _____

_____

More Caring: _____
_____

More Patient: _____
_____

More Accepting: _____
_____

All change has a cost to benefit ratio. Imagine a scale where one side is the cost of changing and the other side is the benefit of changing and doing things differently.

COST   BENEFIT

Common costs to changing can be the uncertainty involved in change, the sense of vulnerability it causes, and feeling like you are more likely to be taken advantage of. However, the benefits of change can include experiencing less stress, feeling and acting more genuine, and having a greater connection to oneself and others. **Describe the costs and benefits of changing as they apply to you:**

Cost: _____

_____

_____

Benefit: _____

_____

_____

STRENGTHENING APPROPRIATE SOCIAL POTENCY

Individuals who are high in social potency are appropriately assertive, decisive, and persuasive. They are likely to influence others, enjoy leadership roles, enjoy being noticed, and enjoy being the center of attention (Tellegen & Waller, 2008). Although this description sounds a great deal like the aspirations that individuals along the narcissistic spectrum have, the reality is that such individuals are inappropriately assertive (aka forceful), usually indecisive, have little persuasive and influential ability, fantasize about leadership roles, hold an unrealistic view of leadership, and love being noticed and the center of attention.

Enhancing social potency is something that clients along the narcissistic spectrum want to do, but their core structure of fear, shame, guilt, doubt, and inferiority distorts their ability to achieve this goal, so they engage in maladaptive behaviors to achieve some semblance that they have done so. To enhance social potency, clients will need to build skills within this domain, and to do so, you will need to explain to them the components of social potency and the steps needed to achieve each component.

NEXT STEPS

Talk to your clients along the narcissistic spectrum about **Strengthening Social Potency** and how they view it. Ask them if they would like to learn skills to enhance it; the odds are very high that they will say "yes." A "no" to this question signals a core structural defense that needs to be addressed before going forward with this activity.

After your client has said "yes," you should discuss the components of social potency, which include assertiveness, decisiveness, persuasive ability, leadership skills, and responding appropriately to recognition. Go over the steps needed to achieve each component, and empower your clients with choice by asking them which one they would like to start with first. Then, walk through the steps, and brainstorm real-world examples that fit with how your clients can implement these skills to achieve their goal of greater social potency.

STRENGTHENING SOCIAL POTENCY

The components to building social potency include assertiveness, decisiveness, persuasive ability, leadership, and responding appropriately to recognition. Each component is listed below, along with the steps needed to achieve success in this area so that you can have a greater impact on your life and the lives of others. Use these steps, and you will see your social potency grow, as well as your ability to influence others in a positive and adaptive way.

ASSERTIVENESS SKILL STEPS

BE FACTUAL AND NON-JUDGMENTAL ABOUT WHAT YOU DO NOT LIKE
Stay focused on the facts, and avoid opinions and judgments.
BE ACCURATE ABOUT THE OUTCOMES OF BEHAVIOR
Focus on the factual outcomes of behavior. Do not exaggerate.
USE "I" STATEMENTS
Use "I" statements to mention your feelings and the impact of the behavior.
LINK THE STEPS
When you link the steps, you pull together the facts, and your statements are more impactful. For example, "I was angry when you came in late and did not tell me." Do not end with, "It felt like *YOU* snuck in."

DECISIVENESS SKILL STEPS

CLEARLY IDENTIFY THE DECISION TO BE MADE
Know what you want to get out of it and what you hope to achieve.

STUDY, STUDY, STUDY
Get as much information as you can.

BRAINSTORM POSSIBLE CHOICES
Determine if the outcomes are consistent with your values, interests, beliefs, and abilities.

BALANCE 3
Ask yourself, "What is the worst that can happen?", "What is the ideal outcome?", and "Can I live with either or neither?"

SELECT OPTIONS AND GATHER INFORMATION
Solicit feedback from trusted others, and be open to possibilities that you have not considered. You do not have to have all the answers – no one does.

DECIDE AND MONITOR
Make your decision, and monitor your results. It is important to recognize that most decisions are more like water than concrete. They are fluid, not solid, and can be changed if necessary.

PERSUASIVE ABILITY SKILL STEPS

KNOW YOUR PURPOSE

Be aware of where you stand and what actual power and influence you have in a situation. Asking for something is less confrontational than demanding something. Persuasive people ask.

LISTEN MORE

Listen actively. Are you receptive to what others have to say? Do you hear objections that need to be resolved? Do you listen for moments of agreement?

HAVE BALANCED OPINIONS

Opinions are shades of gray and not black and white. Acknowledge the other person's opinions and statements of facts, and he or she will do the same for you.

GIVE-AND-TAKE

Be willing to operate a give-and-take relationship. Know you will win some and lose some, and this will enhance your level of being successful over being right.

LET IT GO

Go at the other person's pace, give them space and time to consider, and then let it go. Walk away, and let the facts simmer. Persuasion is a skill equivalent to patience.

THE LAST WORD LOSES

Know your facts, appropriately state the facts, support your view, and ask questions to encourage positive resolution. The one who needs the last word has said too much and usually loses.

LEADERSHIP SKILL STEPS

COMMUNICATE

Clearly and succinctly state your ideas and facts, not opinions. Listen, express empathy, verbalize understanding, be open to alternate views, and discuss issues and concerns.

MOTIVATE

Inspire others by recognizing their skillsets, rewarding their successes, and giving them responsibilities that help them shine. Doing so will help you lead them, and they will want to follow you.

DELEGATE

Delegation is a sign of trust in others. Give tasks that match other's skills, and trust that they will be able to complete them. Be open to assisting them if asked, but do not interfere. Trust yourself.

BE POSITIVE

Encourage a positive environment by asking employees/co-workers about themselves; providing snacks, coffee, and an honest ear when they struggle; and focusing on the upside in times of stress.

BUILDING TRUST

Help others trust that you want to help them by building integrity so that they, in turn, help you. Operate using honesty and ethics as your guide, and you will influence others to do the same.

FLEXIBILITY

Train your brain to have a "go with the flow" outlook. Know your goal, but recognize that it is not always a straightforward path to get there. Allow for unexpected changes, and you will have less stress too.

MANAGING RECOGNITION SKILL STEPS

SAYING THANKS

Be sure that you acknowledge others who helped you achieve your level of recognition. This may seem difficult at times, but saying "thanks" does not equal losing status; rather, it solidifies it.

LET OTHERS SPEAK

Allow others to say things about you that you do well. Hear their words, and allow yourself to feel their appreciation of your work and efforts. Avoid looking for backhanded critiques.

PREEN INTERNALLY

Preening is when you congratulate yourself, and while it is a healthy thing to do, it is important to do so internally. When receiving recognition, approach it with a "thank you" attitude, not one of "I know I'm great."

BE HUMBLE

Humility is the art of modesty. It involves knowing your skills and not overly displaying or talking about them. Your recognition does this, and humility further opens the door to it.

ACCEPT IT

Accept your recognition clearly. Know that others are not tricking you, fooling you, or playing you for a fool. Allow yourself to accept being recognized for a good achievement.

Final Steps

CONCEPTUALIZING SUCCESSFUL TREATMENT

Many mental health providers are frustrated with the process and with their clients along the narcissistic spectrum because of the difficulty conceptualizing treatment goals. Holding the ideal that you will rid the individual of narcissism is not realistic. However, you can change maladaptive patterns into more adaptive ones, and that is considered a therapeutic success. **We all have a degree of narcissism – and there is such thing as healthy narcissism (Kohut, 1971) – but for clients with narcissistic traits, these aspects are distorted and maladaptive.** Therefore, our job as mental health providers is to help these clients learn how to utilize more adaptive traits to get their needs met. In doing so, we lessen the narcissistic expression that causes our clients problems in their personal, professional, academic, and/ or other facets of their lives. How we conceptualize their maladaptive versus adaptive traits and tailor treatment accordingly is a big determinant of treatment success. For example, **the following is a case conceptualization of a client with narcissistic spectrum traits and behaviors**:

RJ is a 22-year-old male, referred for therapy through his workplace Employee Assistance Program (EAP) because he refuses to complete necessary tasks that he feels are beneath him, becomes verbally aggressive when others disagree with him, and engages in behavior to draw attention to himself and away from those he views as "insignificant others." In treatment, you notice an inflated self-image, intense need for admiration and attention, grandiose fantasies, and violent thoughts. You also identify that these problems are being driven by core structure issues involving shame, doubt, and inferiority.

In treatment, if you set your goal to lessen the expression of narcissistic traits and behaviors, you will likely end up frustrated with the process and with RJ. Those goals are too global and unclear. When working with individuals along the narcissistic spectrum, it is important to remind yourself that:

> ### "FOR EVERY SYMPTOM THERE ARE REASONS."
> -Lorna Smith Benjamin (1996, p. 13)

This phrase is by Lorna Smith Benjamin (1996), and it is central to conceptualizing and successfully treating individuals along the narcissistic spectrum. If you examine RJ from this perspective and acknowledge the *reasons* for his narcissistic symptoms and behaviors, his treatment becomes manageable and treatable.

We have to pair his narcissistic core issues with direct and clear adaptive skill building. In treatment, we want to teach RJ to achieve his goals in a more adaptive and healthy manner and recognize the reasons that he does what he does. In the chart below, you will find an example of a successful treatment course with RJ, which includes a depiction of how his core issues result in maladaptive traits, and how these can be met in more adaptive ways. The relevant maladaptive to adaptive components are grayed out to illustrate on which areas to focus in treatment with RJ, as well as the core issues of concern. It is to RJ's benefit to work on his core issues of shame, doubt, and inferiority and to find more adaptive and healthy manifestations.

For example, it is much easier to work with RJ on assertiveness, accurate self-appraisal, reality-based achievements, appreciation of opportunities, self-restraint, and responding with calm and patience than it is to generally try to reduce narcissistic tendencies. Attempting to work on the latter is too global, and many mental health providers attempt to do so but miss the importance of "for every symptom there are reasons" (Benjamin, 1996, p. 13). As a result, they end up feeling angry, frustrated with the process, psychologically abused by their clients, and more.

When you conceptualize successful treatment with your clients along the narcissistic spectrum, you will want to break down the symptoms, look for their underlying reasons or core issues, and focus on skill building in these areas.

Most treatment conceptualizations need to focus on core issues in order to facilitate long-term change in your clients. When you are time-limited, you can address surface structure issues only, with the recognition that this is likely to have a limited impact on your clients and their lives in the long-term. Treatment time limitations include caps imposed by managed care, limited session attendance, and monetary concerns. To achieve long-term change and solidify success with a client like RJ, you need to address core issues and get to the reason that he engages in these behaviors, as opposed to *only* focusing on the behaviors themselves. In the example shown below, we are connecting RJ's narcissistic spectrum core issues with his maladaptive beliefs and traits that can be changed to more adaptive beliefs and traits listed to the right. To learn more about working with core and surface issues for long-term therapeutic change, see the worksheet titled Identifying Surface and Core Structures of Narcissistic Personality Disorder.

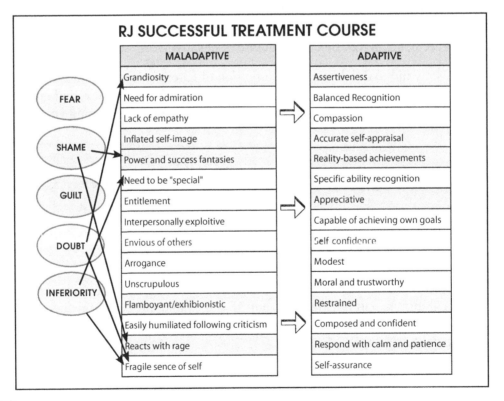

NEXT STEPS:

Use the left side of the next chart to identify your client's core issues and then draw a line to his or her maladaptive narcissistic beliefs or traits, and then follow it across to the related adaptive treatment goals on the right. Using this chart will help you conceptualize areas of treatment more effectively, have greater control over the therapeutic process, and achieve success with clients who were once seen as very challenging.

CONCEPTUALIZING SUCCESSFUL TREATMENT

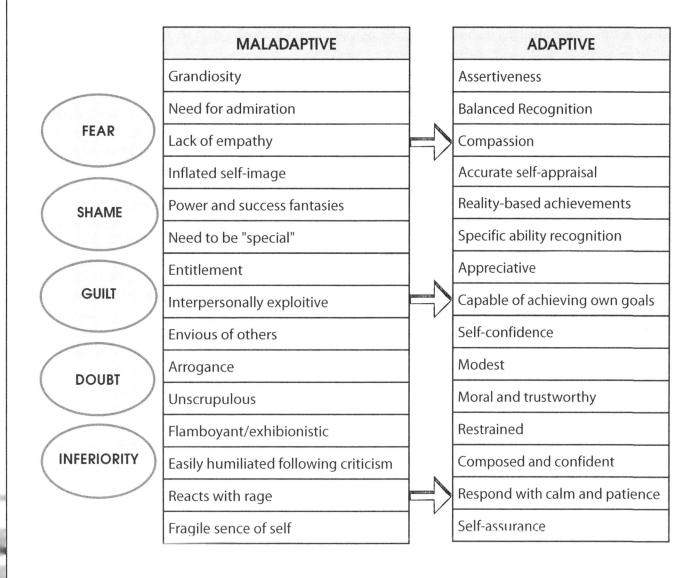

	MALADAPTIVE		ADAPTIVE
FEAR	Grandiosity		Assertiveness
	Need for admiration		Balanced Recognition
	Lack of empathy	→	Compassion
	Inflated self-image		Accurate self-appraisal
SHAME	Power and success fantasies		Reality-based achievements
	Need to be "special"		Specific ability recognition
	Entitlement		Appreciative
GUILT	Interpersonally exploitive	→	Capable of achieving own goals
	Envious of others		Self-confidence
DOUBT	Arrogance		Modest
	Unscrupulous		Moral and trustworthy
	Flamboyant/exhibionistic		Restrained
INFERIORITY	Easily humiliated following criticism		Composed and confident
	Reacts with rage	→	Respond with calm and patience
	Fragile sence of self		Self-assurance

TREATMENT PLANNING FOR SUCCESS

There are many different treatment plan approaches, and they all vary based upon the mental health concerns present in your client. Treatment planning for a client along the narcissistic spectrum is a complex and challenging process. This activity is designed to streamline that process and make it much easier and efficient for you.

There are five parts involved in the development of a successful treatment plan for clients along the narcissistic spectrum:

> 1 = Core structure issues
>
> 2 = Surface structure issues
>
> 3 = Short-term goals
>
> 4 = Long-term goals
>
> 5 = Therapeutic interventions.

Part 1 focuses on core structure issues that are commonly identified in individuals along the narcissistic spectrum. These issues typically include fear, shame, guilt, doubt, and inferiority. It is the mental health provider's job to identify which of these issues are present, the circumstances surrounding their creation, and then develop goals and interventions to address them (see section titled **Identifying Surface and Core Structures of Narcissistic Personality Disorder**).

Part 2 lists common surface structure issues seen in those individuals along the narcissistic spectrum, such as taking advantage of others, reacting to criticism with rage, and excessive feelings of self-importance. You are likely to see these issues manifest in treatment because they are on the surface and exposed. However, it is counterproductive to attempt to attenuate each of these issues individually. Doing so adds an unnecessary level of frustration for the mental health provider, as well as the client, because surface issues in these individuals do not extinguish without addressing the underlying cause, core issue. However, some mental health providers may only be able to address surface structure issues as a result of session limits imposed by insurance, monetary concerns of the client, etc. In these cases, some relief and skill building is better than nothing, but it is likely to be limited in the long-term because core issues continue to be problematic and drive surface structure issues and patterns.

Part 3 identifies common short-term goals that increase the probability of treatment success and entail specific skill building. This process is likely to require approximately 12-18 sessions, depending on where the individual is along the narcissistic spectrum. These short-term goals can include honestly approaching situations and others involved in achieving goals, verbalizing feelings of frustration to appropriate others prior to acting out, and initiating and responding to others in an honest and straightforward manner. To achieve these goals, the mental health provider would focus on social skills training, teaching clients to accurately assess the world and the role that they play in various situations, and identifying and overcoming challenges. Short-term goals do not include addressing the roots of the behavior (i.e., core structure) but, rather, focus on directly lessening or controlling the problematic behaviors that are causing clients difficulty across a variety of domains.

Part 4 identifies common long-term goals toward which to work in treatment. It is important to remember that the core structure is well protected so you will need to identify defenses employed by your client, prepare for them, and develop counter strategies to mitigate their disruption throughout the treatment process. If you are interested in learning more about common defenses employed by those along the narcissistic spectrum, see Part II and III of this workbook, as well as *Narcissism Key Target Areas for Treatment* (Fox, 2015, pp. 87-88). Addressing and reducing the influence of the core structure takes time, as it took years to develop and usually takes years to counter and learn adaptive methods to get those core needs met. You will notice that these goals appear more global in nature, but they are specifically attuned to those core structure issues, such as reducing the intensity of fear, shame, guilt, doubt, and inferiority; increasing the degree of insight needed to accurately assess others; and improving interpersonal skills and frustration tolerance.

Finally, **Part 5** includes a list of common therapeutic interventions that can be utilized to address both surface and core structural issues to achieve these short-term and long-term goals. Examine the list to see which interventions fit your style and which do not. For any interventions with which you are unfamiliar, try to learn more about them through seminars or trainings so that you can expand your approach, given that working with individuals along the narcissistic spectrum is challenging and unique. However, it is a highly rewarding experience when you connect with them, help them grow beyond their pathology, and watch them approach the world in a healthier and more adaptive manner.

NEXT STEPS

Use the **Treatment Plan** worksheet at the end of this chapter to create a successful plan. Information pertaining to each part of the process is provided in the following **Clinician Resources** to help you fill out the Treatment Plan Form. On the Treatment Plan Form, identify the problem that your client is having in concrete terms. Stating that he or she is experiencing difficulty as a result of narcissistic pathology is not specific enough and will cause confusion and misdirection in your treatment trajectory.

You can look at Part 1 or 2 to help you identify presenting problems; it is okay to list the same issue twice when creating a treatment plan. Use the information in Parts 1 and 2 to help you identify issues pertaining to personality structure and issues. Part 3 will help you identify applicable short-term goals, and Part 4 will help you recognize long-term goals. Part 5 lists therapeutic inventions for you to include on the worksheet.

At the conclusion of this worksheet, you will see a box for "what has worked" and "what has *not* worked." These boxes are provided so the mental health provider can examine interventions and approaches that did and did not fit for this particular client. With most individuals along the narcissistic spectrum, the mental health provider will have to utilize a fluid approach by adding interventions that work and removing those that have never worked, or those that no longer work, as the client develops. Working with any individual along a personality disorder spectrum is going to require a fluid approach to achieve success; it is one of those intrinsic factors that adds to the complexity of successful treatment planning and attainment.

CLINICIAN RESOURCES

1. Core structure issues:

FEAR　　SHAME　　GUILT　　DOUBT　　INFERIORITY

2. Surface structure issues:

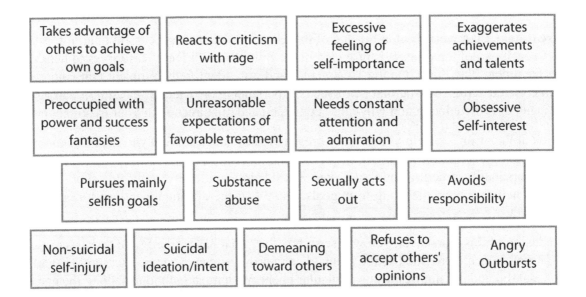

Takes advantage of others to achieve own goals	Reacts to criticism with rage	Excessive feeling of self-importance	Exaggerates achievements and talents
Preoccupied with power and success fantasies	Unreasonable expectations of favorable treatment	Needs constant attention and admiration	Obsessive Self-interest
Pursues mainly selfish goals	Substance abuse	Sexually acts out	Avoids responsibility
Non-suicidal self-injury	Suicidal ideation/intent	Demeaning toward others	Refuses to accept others' opinions	Angry Outbursts

3. Short-term goals:

1. Honestly approach situations and others involved in achieving goals.

2. Verbalize feelings of frustration to appropriate others prior to acting out.

3. Initiate and respond to others in an honest and straightforward manner.

4. Remove self from situations that trigger anger and frustration.

5. Build accurate insight into one's value in various situations and relationships.

6. Accurately convey one's achievements based upon facts and the role that one plays in work and social interactions.

7. Accurately assess the world and the role that one plays in various situations.

8. Create an achievement plan to attain desired goals that are consistent with one's abilities and interests.

9. Enhance assessment skills to evaluate work or social situations.

10. Become comfortable being alone and with self.

11. Recognize and build the value of others based on clear assessment of their strengths and weaknesses.

12. Develop goals based upon a team approach and/or to the benefit of others that do not have immediate and transparent benefits to self.

13. Manage sexual impulses and relationships with balance and regard for others' needs as well as for self.

14. Acknowledge and accept responsibility for reactions and behaviors.

15. Develop a non-suicidal self-injury and/or suicide prevention plan to avoid harming self.

16. Avoid using terms and phrases that belittle, degrade, manipulate, hurt, and demean others.

17. Openly accept the opinions of others and develop strategies to weigh the honest value of those opinions and their impact on self.

18. Develop reality-based thinking and assessment that fosters positive feelings about self, others, the world, and the future.

19. Articulate feelings in an honest and straightforward manner, and assess appropriate times and places to do so.

20. If prescribed medication, maintain medication compliance and routine visits with doctors.

21. Agree to attend therapy sessions even when overt and severe distress is present.

4. Long-term goals:

1. Reduce overall intensity of feelings of inferiority, shame, doubt, guilt, and fear.

2. Increase the degree of insight needed to accurately assess others.

3. Improve interpersonal skills and frustration tolerance.

4. Solidify anger management techniques to accurately assess and respond to distressing situations.

5. Develop reality-based assessment of one's achievements and goal attainment.

6. Enhance self-esteem to interact with others in an authentic manner.

7. Accurately assess strengths and weakness in self and others.

8. Demonstrate improved relationship stability by maintaining honest and transparent self-expression.

9. Maintain abstinence from substances that adversely impact functioning and the ability to cope with stress.

10. Acknowledge stress and frustration associated with one's role in difficult situations.

5. Treatment interventions:

Mindfulness	Thought stopping	Applied behavior analysis
Anger management	Exposure	Biofeedback
Relaxation techniques	Individual therapy	Journaling
Hypnotherapy	Social skills training	Emotional regulation
Family systems approach	Interpersonal effectiveness	Narrative therapy
Motivational interviewing	Art therapy	Group therapy – specific to issue being addressed
Solution-focused therapy	Systematic desensitization	Cognitive-behavioral therapy
Cost/benefit analysis	Distress tolerance skills	Cognitive restructuring
Nightmare exposure and rescripting	Progressive muscle relaxation	Self-compassion letter

TREATMENT PLAN FORM

Presenting Problem: _____
_____
_____

Core Structure (motivators)**:** _____
_____
_____

Surface Structure (behaviors, moods, etc.)**:** _____
_____
_____

Short-term goals: _____
_____
_____

Long-term goals: _____
_____
_____

Treatment interventions: _____
_____
_____

What **has** worked	What **has _not_** worked
_____	_____
_____	_____
_____	_____
_____	_____
_____	_____

Section 2

Treating **The Partner**
of a *Narcissist*

Setting the Stage for Successful Treatment

WHAT IS AND WHAT MAY NEVER BE AND CHALLENGING FOUNDATIONAL BELIEFS

Relationship expectations are central to relationship satisfaction and composed of foundational beliefs to sustain the relationship. Most individuals in a relationship with someone along the narcissistic spectrum have usually given up or completely foregone the idea of getting those expectations met. The individual begins to develop compensations to counter and manage the loss of those expectations by creating distortions of the relationship. These distortions and/or compensations are usually rationalizations for the continuance of the relationship. These individuals usually end up in treatment because the dissonance between what they want from the relationship and what they are receiving is growing. This activity is designed to help your clients define their relationship expectations and honestly and clearly examine if their significant other meets those expectations.

NEXT STEPS

Give clients the **Relationship Expectations Questionnaire** and ask them to answer each item as honestly as possible. Ask clients to answer without censoring, evaluating, or being fearful of what their significant other might think of the results. There are no right or wrong answers. Honest responses are critical to exploring relationship expectations, learning more about your client's significant other, and setting the stage for successful treatment.

After your client has completed the questionnaire, add up the results, and use the response categories below to assess if your client's expectations in the relationship are being met, some or few are being met, or none are being met. When you go over the results with your client, be sure to pay attention to any responses rated 3 through 5, as these are indicative of areas for future focus in treatment. If you get nothing but 1s and 2s, you may want to challenge or educate your client on relationship distortions.

Scoring the Relationship Expectations Questionnaire:

Add up the scores as they correspond to the 19 questions on the **Relationship Expectations Questionnaire**, and compare your results to the response categories below. Use these results to help assess the relationship, the expectations, and the distorted or non-distorted view of the individual with whom your client is in a relationship.

Meets expectations	1 – 32
Meets some or few expectations	33 – 63
Does not meet expectations	64 – 95

RELATIONSHIP EXPECTATIONS QUESTIONNAIRE

Please read each statement and description. Statements are bolded, followed by a brief description of each statement in parentheses. Rate how strongly you agree or disagree with each statement as it applies to your relationship with your significant other. After you have completed the questionnaire, bring it back to your therapist for scoring and to discuss the results.

1. **We can talk openly and honestly about our thoughts and feelings.** (You can talk to one another honestly without fear of upsetting each another or your partner leaving.)

   ① Strongly Agree   ② Agree   ③ Neither   ④ Disagree   ⑤ Strongly Disagree

2. **We can have healthy disagreements and do not have to "stuff it" in** (To "stuff it" in means to hold in your feelings to avoid disagreements and to prevent perceived emotional or literal abandonment. Stuffing it leads to apathy, which causes dispirited relationship involvement).

   ① Strongly Agree   ② Agree   ③ Neither   ④ Disagree   ⑤ Strongly Disagree

3. **It is okay to have separate passions and for my partner to still support me** (Divergence of interests is a healthy thing and creates a positive sense of self and feelings of support. Failure to have this divergence causes confusion and codependency).

   ① Strongly Agree   ② Agree   ③ Neither   ④ Disagree   ⑤ Strongly Disagree

4. **I feel safe when showing vulnerability** (If you mention fears or anxieties, you are not ridiculed for it. The issue is examined not as a character flaw but, rather, as an issue separate from who *you* are).

   ① Strongly Agree   ② Agree   ③ Neither   ④ Disagree   ⑤ Strongly Disagree

5. **Relationship excitement is not required at all times** (It is okay to have slow-paced and calm moments in a relationship. This builds intimacy and comfort with yourself and your partner).

① Strongly Agree   ② Agree   ③ Neither   ④ Disagree   ⑤ Strongly Disagree

6. **I am okay being me!** (Your partner does not try to change or mold you into who *they* want you to be. Rather, you are accepted for being you).

① Strongly Agree   ② Agree   ③ Neither   ④ Disagree   ⑤ Strongly Disagree

7. **Little things are as important as the big ones** (Ordinary moments or small gestures are recognized and appreciated. Every gift does not have to be a Ferrari).

① Strongly Agree   ② Agree   ③ Neither   ④ Disagree   ⑤ Strongly Disagree

8. **We can agree to disagree** (You will not agree with everyone all of the time, no matter who it is. This difference is seen as okay and accepted, and even encouraged, in your relationship).

① Strongly Agree   ② Agree   ③ Neither   ④ Disagree   ⑤ Strongly Disagree

9. **During times of success or failure, my partner is still there** (Your significant other is there during hard times and good times; support is a marathon, not a sprint).

① Strongly Agree   ② Agree   ③ Neither   ④ Disagree   ⑤ Strongly Disagree

10. **I trust myself and my partner** (Your partner trusts you, and you trust him or her. You do not need to check your partner's phone, email, social media, etc. to find out what s/he is *really* thinking).

① Strongly Agree   ② Agree   ③ Neither   ④ Disagree   ⑤ Strongly Disagree

11. **I receive appropriate expression of affection from my partner** (Your partner expresses feelings through words, behavior, or both at a level that is consistent with how s/he feels about you).

①	②	③	④	⑤
Strongly Agree	Agree	Neither	Disagree	Strongly Disagree

12. **My partner makes time for me** (Your partner makes time during the day to connect with you verbally, physically, or both. You feel like a priority in the list of things that make up each day).

①	②	③	④	⑤
Strongly Agree	Agree	Neither	Disagree	Strongly Disagree

13. **I receive consistent compassion during good times and bad** (Your partner shows concern during trying times and difficulties. S/he helps you up if you fall, literally and figuratively).

①	②	③	④	⑤
Strongly Agree	Agree	Neither	Disagree	Strongly Disagree

14. **I am respected by my partner** (Boundaries, values, words, beliefs, and actions are accepted without ridicule or "just jokes." Who you are is accepted and understood from your perspective without having to change in order to maintain the relationship).

①	②	③	④	⑤
Strongly Agree	Agree	Neither	Disagree	Strongly Disagree

15. **Consideration for me and empathy are present in my relationship** (Your partner thinks about how something might impact you positively or negatively. S/he takes time to see the world through your eyes and experience).

①	②	③	④	⑤
Strongly Agree	Agree	Neither	Disagree	Strongly Disagree

16. **My partner likes me** (Your partner expresses interest in you and genuinely appears to like who you are and all that comes with it).

①	②	③	④	⑤
Strongly Agree	Agree	Neither	Disagree	Strongly Disagree

17. **Sex is positive, open, accepted, and genuine** (The physical connection between you and your significant other is positive, open, accepted, and genuine. It is not "sky rockets in flight" each time, but a physical linking with someone else).

①	②	③	④	⑤
Strongly Agree	Agree	Neither	Disagree	Strongly Disagree

18. **My partner shows me selflessness** (Your partner demonstrates the ability to be kind and generous. S/he incurs a suitable degree of inconvenience or discomfort for your betterment even though there is no clear benefit for him or her).

①	②	③	④	⑤
Strongly Agree	Agree	Neither	Disagree	Strongly Disagree

19. **We are able to have intimacy beyond sexual connection** (This is *not* sex. It refers to the ability to connect on many levels and achieve a sense of closeness that encompasses all of the other factors on this list without giving up, sacrificing, and/or apologizing for who you are).

①	②	③	④	⑤
Strongly Agree	Agree	Neither	Disagree	Strongly Disagree

IDENTIFYING THE NARCISSISTIC SELF-SERVING SIGNIFICANT OTHER

Individuals along the narcissistic spectrum are often in relationships of varying degrees of codependency, as well as relationships characterized by verbal, physical, and mental abuse. As mental health providers, our clients are often significant others of someone with narcissistic traits, and they seek therapy because they are experiencing conflict with their narcissistic counterpart. We have to design treatment inroads to provide the best treatment possible to help our clients in these relationships. This exercise is designed to help clients who are in a relationship with an individual along the narcissistic spectrum to build insight so that they can make clear decisions about staying in the relationship, managing negative/adverse aspects of the relationship, or leaving the relationship to better themselves.

This exercise can be used with an individual client or in a couples session. The Relationship Identifiers Form can help clarify the relationship for both partners, as well identify common grounds for dysfunction and opposite viewpoints in the relationship. The goal in the couples session is the same as it is in the individual session: to build insight so that both of your clients can make clear and empowered decisions about working on the relationship or dissolving it.

NEXT STEPS

Provide your clients with the **Relationship Identifiers Form**, and ask them to complete it as openly and honestly as they can. Ask them to answer each statement without evaluating their responses or worrying what anyone else might think of the responses. If this is a couples exercise, you may want to clarify what will happen after each partner completes the form. For example, will they compare answers, will they exchange sheets so the other can see how his/her partner identifies the relationship, or are the responses just for the therapist to see to help determine commonalities and differences in how each partner identifies the relationship?

It is always a good idea to set ground rules first about reactions to the answers. Many responses are going to upset the other person, so it is important to clarify that yelling, using answers as ammunition to hurt the other person, and physical violence are unacceptable and not the objective of this exercise.

Follow-up: You can ask your client, or the couple, to go home and write up clear examples of those items marked "True" in order to further explore the relationship. It is important that these examples be sufficiently clear that even an observer who has never met the couple could agree that the example illustrates the relationship identifier statement.

RELATIONSHIP IDENTIFIERS FORM

Below are several relationship identifiers. Answer each statement by marking (√) whether it is true or false with regard to your significant other, the relationship, or how you feel or have felt in the relationship. You cannot choose both answers, only true or false. Once you are finished, go over the form with your therapist to help identify areas of concern in your relationship. The goal of this exercise is to build your level of insight into the relationship so that you can make clearer and healthier decisions.

Your partner lies often, even when confronted with undeniable proof.	☐ TRUE	☐ FALSE
Disagreements and arguments are often turned on you, and you are made to feel at fault for asking for something that you need or want in the relationship.	☐ TRUE	☐ FALSE
Your partner has creative, confusing arguments used to justify unjustifiable decisions or situations.	☐ TRUE	☐ FALSE
You often feel caught between your significant other and your family, friends, or coworkers and are made to feel guilty about it.	☐ TRUE	☐ FALSE
Your partner often calls others, or you, names, such as stupid, idiot, jerk, moron, etc.	☐ TRUE	☐ FALSE
You have become hyper-vigilant about your own behavior out of fear of disappointing your partner.	☐ TRUE	☐ FALSE
Your partner often manipulates you into doing things that you really do not want to do in order to please him/her.	☐ TRUE	☐ FALSE
Blame for your partner's behavior is often placed on you without just cause or clear reasoning.	☐ TRUE	☐ FALSE
Your partner can be very charming and attractive to get his/her needs and wants met.	☐ TRUE	☐ FALSE
Your partner sees him/herself as unique, special, and deserving of praise, though his/her deeds do not clearly match this view.	☐ TRUE	☐ FALSE
You spend considerable time worrying about your partner's needs while sacrificing your own.	☐ TRUE	☐ FALSE

You feel that you have surrendered yourself to the relationship so that your partner can be happy and content.	☐ **TRUE**	☐ **FALSE**
Your partner does not treat you like a person, but an object.	☐ **TRUE**	☐ **FALSE**
You feel like property as opposed to another human being.	☐ **TRUE**	☐ **FALSE**
Your partner often says one thing and does another to get his/her needs or wants met.	☐ **TRUE**	☐ **FALSE**
When you confront your partner, you receive ultimatums or uncompromising demands to meet or you will suffer the loss of the relationship.	☐ **TRUE**	☐ **FALSE**
You try to stay one-step ahead of your partner's lies or manipulations.	☐ **TRUE**	☐ **FALSE**
If you say something and hurt your partner, the response is rage, playing the victim, or your partner disappears.	☐ **TRUE**	☐ **FALSE**
Your partner rarely mentions the needs or concerns of others.	☐ **TRUE**	☐ **FALSE**
Your partner will take opportunities to get ahead whenever possible.	☐ **TRUE**	☐ **FALSE**
Your partner tries to restrict your contact with family, friends, and coworkers.	☐ **TRUE**	☐ **FALSE**
Your partner never seems to have enough of you.	☐ **TRUE**	☐ **FALSE**
Your partner is very argumentative when confronted with opinions and views that do not agree with his/her own.	☐ **TRUE**	☐ **FALSE**
Your partner likes an audience and attention most of the time.	☐ **TRUE**	☐ **FALSE**
Your partner has a singular focus on his/her own needs and wants, even at the expense of others or you.	☐ **TRUE**	☐ **FALSE**

SHOULD I STAY OR SHOULD I GO?

Partners in relationships with individuals along the narcissistic spectrum often come to treatment because of dissonance they are experiencing in the relationship and ambivalence as to whether they should stay or go. This is a complex issue from the viewpoint of the mental health provider, as well as the client. Working to identify why the individual is tethered to the relationship is often challenging work, but it is critical to help the client decide if the relationship is one to maintain or dissolve. This exercise will help to challenge clients to see the relationship honestly and their role within it.

As clients increase insight into their relationship, and dissonance subsequently increases, they can use that tension to make changes, self-motivate, and move forward. By doing so, they can address and change maladaptive patterns, dig deeper into their motivations for staying in the relationship, and reduce symptoms that keep them stuck in relationships with individuals along the narcissistic spectrum.

NEXT STEPS

Provide clients with the **Relationship Balance Sheet**. Ask them to mark the boxes that represent their relationship and their place within it. Once it is completed, go over each item and try to identify a theme. For example, did they only mark items that reflect the power and control of the individual along the narcissistic spectrum, or did they mark items that illustrate their sense of self-worth and their belief that they deserve to be treated better? Items on the left pertain to self-empowerment and overcoming issues individuals typically deal with as a result of being in a relationship with an individual along the narcissistic spectrum. Items on the right refer to factors that keep them in the relationship, which are related to an unhealthy dependence on the relationship and illustrate that they have little self-esteem and power in the relationship.

Some clients may choose the item on the left *and* the item on the right. This is not a surprising result, as many individuals are in conflict about their relationship. In these cases, examine the areas of conflict, determine what is lying underneath those areas, such as self-esteem issues, abandonment, fear of loneliness, etc., and identify those areas that are not in conflict to help move clients forward.

This exercise can open up many avenues to explore with your client about relationships, what keeps them in them, and what it would take for them to move themselves forward.

THE RELATIONSHIP BALANCE SHEET

The Relationship Balance Sheet is designed to help you identify the reasons that you continue to stay in your relationship. Mark (√) the items that fit your reasons for maintaining or dissolving the relationship. It is ok to mark some responses that appear on opposite ends, such as "There is someone better out there for me" and "No one else will love me," because sometimes people feel caught between the two extremes.

Answer as honestly as you can, without editing your thoughts. Once you are finished, go over your responses with your therapist. This exercise is designed to build insight into your relationship so that you can make healthy choices for yourself and your relationship.

Relationship Balance Sheet	
☐ There is someone better out there for me.	☐ No one else will love me.
☐ I deserve to be treated better.	☐ My partner gives me what I deserve.
☐ I should be treated like the passionate and able person that I am.	☐ I am unlovable and inadequate.
☐ Being single only means that I am taking care of me, and that is a good thing.	☐ I am ashamed to be alone.
☐ If I accept the person that my partner is today, I need more and better.	☐ I can change my partner to make this relationship perfect.
☐ I deserve someone who treats me like the unique and special person I am.	☐ I do not like myself, so I am with someone who treats me like they do not like me either.
☐ I want to determine my own success, and I have nothing to prove to anyone.	☐ I have to please my partner to prove that I am not a failure.
☐ I see value in working to build a relationship that grows from my effort and does not stay stuck.	☐ Walking away is too hard; it is easier just to stay.
☐ Time is not enough to warrant commitment in a relationship that hurts.	☐ We have been together for so long, and I have invested too much.
☐ I deserve to feel like a priority.	☐ My own needs are secondary and my partner's happiness is more important.

☐ It is okay for me to define my own boundaries and discover myself.	☐ I am not sure where I end and my partner starts. If I leave, I lose myself.
☐ I am responsible for my own feelings.	☐ If I end the relationship, I will hurt my partner's feelings.
☐ My partner is old enough and able enough to take care of him/herself.	☐ There is no one else to take care of my partner if I were to leave.
☐ Focusing on myself and meeting my own needs has value.	☐ My partner makes me feel needed, and I need to feel needed.
☐ As an adult, people have to fix and take responsibility for their own lives.	☐ There is no one else to take responsibility and help my partner if I am not there.
☐ The only person that I can truly control is myself, and that is enough.	☐ I have a sense of control over my partner.
☐ Fear will not keep me from feeling satisfied.	☐ It is easier to stay with what I know than try something new.
☐ When I look objectively at this relationship, happiness is more fantasy than reality.	☐ I have a beautiful picture of how our life will be one day.
☐ Being alone is a sign of strength that opens doors to opportunity.	☐ If I am alone, I am worthless.
☐ I can choose my own path and destination, determined by me.	☐ If not for my partner, I would be nowhere.

HOW I (WE) SEE IT

Many clients in relationships with individuals along the narcissistic spectrum are often overwhelmed and confused by their feelings, thoughts, and/or behaviors related to why they stay, why they tolerate the abuse and mistreatment, what keeps them in the relationship, what they get out of the relationship, etc., and this can be attributed to how they see themselves, how they see their partner, and how they see their relationship. Many adults are not very skilled at articulating their feelings, thoughts, and/or behaviors in a clear and concise manner, and this can be an impediment to treatment, but asking them to draw can overcome this. There is immense benefit in asking adults to draw, but many mental health providers think of it as only useful for children who cannot fully express themselves.

The following exercise is a drawing technique. It is not an art test but an activity that is intended to be a means of expression. The goal of this activity is to help your client and his or her partner who is along the narcissistic spectrum (if the partner is participating in treatment) conceptualize how they see themselves, each other, the relationship, and the successful end to treatment. By having them participate in this activity, the mental health provider is given an opportunity to see what the client and the client's partner see.

NEXT STEPS

Provide clients with all **four of the next sheets** for this activity, and ask them (and their partner if he or she is participating) to draw the following: themselves within the relationship currently, their partner, the relationship, and themselves and the relationship at the end of successful treatment. Remind clients not to worry about their drawing ability, as this is not an art test, but a means to express their perspective. This activity can be completed in session or as homework.

Once the activity is completed, ask your client, and his or her partner (if present), about their drawings, what it was like to complete this activity, and what different parts of the drawings mean to them. Some additional questions can be: What did you want to convey by the drawings? What do you hope that your partner takes away from this activity? Did you find it easier to draw these aspects of the relationship than to verbalize them? If, after participating in the activity, clients say that they still prefer to verbalize these aspects of the relationship, ask them to do so in the spaces provided as well.

The mental health provider should examine the drawings and look for themes (e.g., sad or dismal themes), such as the size of the client, individuals or aspects that might be missing, and whether the drawing is simplistic or complex in nature. The mental health provider should also assess how clients felt when drawing themselves, their partner, and their relationship. It is also important to assess how clients think their partner would feel seeing the drawing and to ask if anything held them or their partner (if present) back from fully expressing themselves.

Interpreting drawings can be difficult and a complex process. This exercise is designed to help you gain insight into your clients, their partners, and their relationship. This is not designed as an assessment measure and should not be used as such. If you enjoy this technique, there are many continuing education opportunities that focus on art therapy and interpretation.

ME WITHIN MY RELATIONSHIP

Draw how you see yourself within your relationship. Do not hold back, and draw as much or as little detail as you feel comfortable. This is not an art test, but a drawing activity.

MY PARTNER

Draw how you see your partner. Do not hold back, and draw as much or as little detail as you feel comfortable. This is not an art test, but a drawing activity.

MY RELATIONSHIP

Draw how you see your relationship. Do not hold back, and draw as much or as little detail as you feel comfortable. This is not an art test, but a drawing activity.

ME AND MY RELATIONSHIP AT
THE END OF SUCCESSFUL TREATMENT

Draw how you see yourself and your relationship at the end of treatment when you have achieved your goals. Do not hold back, and draw as much or as little detail as you feel comfortable. This is not an art test, but a drawing activity.

Addressing and Changing Maladaptive Patterns

BREAKING THE CYCLE OF GLORIFYING, BELITTLING, AND ABANDONING

A common issue in relationships with individuals who are along the narcissistic spectrum is the cyclical experience of:

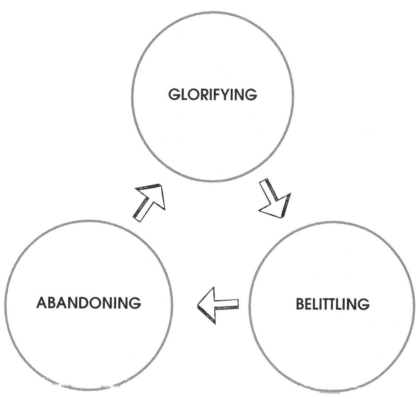

The cycle of glorifying, belittling, and abandoning creates an emotional system that perpetuates itself to the point where the partner loses his or her sense of efficacy and/or self-control. When a relationship begins with an individual along the narcissistic spectrum, all of the stories and presentations seem so impressive that the individual is glorified, and the partner tends to feel as though he or she has met someone magical and that he or she has found his or her "soul mate." This phase of the relationship is called the glorifying phase. During the glorifying phase, the individual along the narcissistic spectrum gives the identified partner all that he or she desires, such as attention, sex, elaborate trips and gifts, and whispers of a perfect future together.

This phase does not last long, and the attention, sex, trips, gifts, and painting of a perfect future begin to diminish. Red flags begin to appear in the form of subtle, or not so subtle, micro-abusive jabs, such as degrading language, demeaning comments, withholding affection and emotional expression, and gaslighting (e.g., a form of psychological abuse where the abuser manipulates someone into questioning his or her own reality, memory, or perception; see the activity on **Contending with Gaslighting** for more information).

The individual along the narcissistic spectrum will then disappear and abandon the partner, physically and/or emotionally. The partner is usually the one who is seen as having failed and is blamed by the individual along the narcissistic spectrum for any problems and the now broken relationship. Being discarded sends the partner into a frenzy to restore what was once so seemingly perfect, beautiful, and fulfilling. The individual along the narcissistic spectrum takes the partner back, but with conditions. When the relationship resumes, there are smatterings of the good times, which are just enough to keep the partner present and invested. A lesser form of glorifying is present but enough to keep the partner hooked and along for the ride. The cycle then repeats in which the partner again engages in belittling, then abandoning, and so forth. This unhealthy relationship pattern can continue for years or decades in some cases.

It is important for mental health providers to be aware of this pattern and to help clients increase their awareness of it and to use methods to block these maladaptive patterns that are so harmful.

NEXT STEPS

Provide your client with the **My Relationship Cycle** worksheets. These can be filled out in session or as homework. The first part entails asking the client to identify if the relationship has the components of glorifying, belittling, and abandoning. If so, ask your client to place a large X in the box(es) provided. The boxes are large so that clients can clearly see that they acknowledge the presence of these issues. The last box is included to allow your clients to recognize that this cycle exists and that it is not a one-time issue. If this cycle has occurred once, it is likely thematic in your client's life.

In the next section, clients will identify instances of glorifying, belittling, and abandoning by providing clear instances of how these issues manifest. In the final part of this exercise, clients answer "yes" or "no" questions regarding what keeps them stuck in the cycle. It is followed by questions to help them challenge glorifying, belittling, and abandoning behaviors and to teach them how to untether themselves from this cycle of relationship abuse. If your client marks "no" for all of the questions, you may want to revisit the relationship, clarify the relationship cycle and their role within it.

It is very beneficial for clients to be cognizant of these issues by writing out how they can overcome them and empower themselves to prevent the cycle from occurring. Increasing this awareness is a great start to working with a client who wants to break out of the cycle of abuse often seen in relationships with individuals who are along the narcissistic spectrum.

MY RELATIONSHIP CYCLE

Below are descriptors of the glorifying, belittling, and abandoning cycle that is often seen in many relationships with individuals along the narcissistic spectrum. Go through each step and place a large X in the box if your relationship has components of the glorifying, belittling, and abandoning cycle. Next, clearly identify instances in your relationship that pertain to each stage, and then answer critical questions about yourself and this abusive cycle.

Finally, answer questions to challenge glorifying, belittling, and abandoning behaviors so that you do not have to be tied to this relationship cycle. Breaking this cycle is not an easy thing to do, and working with your therapist is critical so that he or she can provide support and insight along the way. You can break this cycle.

Place a large X in the box if your relationship has the component of the glorifying, belittling, and/or abandoning cycle.

☐ **Glorifying**	When we first met, my partner was full of exciting stories, experiences, and approached life with passion and shared this with me. We clicked emotionally, and s/he felt like my "soul mate." The relationship had everything anyone could want: attention, sex, elaborate trips and gifts, and whispers of a perfect future together.
☐ **Belittling**	Eventually, routine set in, and the attention, sex, trips, gifts, and painting of a perfect future diminished. Red flags began to appear in the form of subtle jabs, such as degrading language, demeaning comments, withholding of affection, and manipulation to the point that I questioned my own reality, memory, or perception.
☐ **Abandoning**	My partner began to disappear, and the feeling of abandonment arose. My partner blamed me for the problems in the relationship and the now broken relationship. I felt a sense of frenzy to restore the relationship that once was seemingly perfect, beautiful, and fulfilling. My partner took me back, but with conditions. When the relationship resumed, there were reminders of the good times, just enough to keep me present and invested. My partner continued to engage in a lesser form of glorifying, but enough to keep me hooked and along for the ride.
☐ Cycle Continues…	

Clearly identify instances of glorifying in your relationship. You can use all three spaces or write on the back of this worksheet if you have more than three.

1. _____

   _____

2. _____

   _____

3. _____

   _____

Clearly identify instances of belittling in your relationship. You can use all three spaces or write on the back of this worksheet if you have more than three.

1. _____

   _____

2. _____

   _____

3. _____

   _____

Clearly identify instances of abandoning in your relationship. You can use all three spaces or write on the back of this worksheet if you have more than three.

1. _____

   _____

2. _____

   _____

3. _____

   _____

To start to overcome the glorifying stage, you have to examine those qualities and experiences and ask yourself:

☐ YES ☐ NO   Is my partner giving me something that I am missing?

☐ YES ☐ NO   Is this something that I can give myself?

☐ YES ☐ NO   Can I empower myself to meet my own needs and expectations?

☐ YES ☐ NO   Can I look at my relationship objectively and clearly?

☐ YES ☐ NO   Do I glorify my partner to overcome my own shame, doubt, and wounds?

1. **I will give myself what I need by:** _____

_____

_____

2. **I will empower myself by:** _____

_____

_____

3. **I will overcome my shame, doubt, and wounds by:** _____

_____

_____

To start to overcome the belittling stage, you have to examine those instances and experiences and ask yourself:

☐ YES ☐ NO   Do I deserve to be spoken to with respect at all times?

☐ YES ☐ NO   Would I be okay with someone belittling my friend the way that I am belittled in my relationship?

☐ YES ☐ NO   Can I challenge the red flags that I see?

☐ YES ☐ NO   Do I deserve respect and attention that makes me feel good about myself?

☐ YES ☐ NO   Is there anything that would be so demeaning or belittling that it would warrant ending the relationship? If yes, what is it:

_____

_____

_____

1. **When someone speaks to me disrespectfully, I will:** _____

_____

_____

2. **I will challenge the red flags I see by:** _____

_____

_____

3. **When I feel belittled, I am going to:** _____

_____

_____

To start to overcome the abandoning stage, you have to examine and ask yourself:

☐ YES ☐ NO   Will I be okay if the relationship ends?

☐ YES ☐ NO   Do I believe that once I am alone, I will always be alone?

☐ YES ☐ NO   Do I need to take 100% of the responsibility for the relationship's success or failure?

☐ YES ☐ NO   Can I see a future without this person in my life?

☐ YES ☐ NO   Can I accept myself and be self-reliant?

1. **If the relationship ends, I am going to:** _____

_____

_____

2. **My responsibility in the relationship includes:** _____

_____

_____

3. **Being more self-reliant and accepting of myself involves:** _____

_____

_____

CLARIFYING AND MAINTAINING BOUNDARIES

Having boundaries is a very scary thing for those in relationships with individuals along the narcissistic spectrum. Boundaries mean setting standards and qualifiers or, in some cases, letting go of those standards and qualifiers to continue the relationship. Boundaries are a topic that will be revisited time and time again throughout the therapy process, as setting boundaries is critical in order for these clients to be able to do things differently in their relationship and in their lives.

In resetting boundaries that were once diffuse, clients can typically expect resistance, given that those in their world are used to having them do what others want. By developing, defining, implementing, and holding true to adaptive boundaries you are empowering your client to create a psychologically healthier lifestyle characterized by less anxiety, depression, and other surface structure issues your client typically has to manage.

There are four types of boundaries discussed in this exercise: *Solid, Broken, Loose, and Adaptable*. Knowing what type of boundary is present and how to move from maladaptive boundaries to adaptive boundaries will be the focus of this exercise. A graphical representation of the planet Earth, which represents your client's world, surrounded by each type of boundary is presented below.

NEXT STEPS

Provide clients with the **My Boundaries and Beyond** activity sheets. Ask clients to read each type of boundary and indicate which boundaries they possess. It is possible to have different boundaries with different people and in different situations. If clients indicate that they have more than one type of boundary, try to identify which boundary is most salient and relevant to their relationship with the individual along the narcissistic spectrum. After identifying which type of boundary is most relevant, clients will then describe this boundary and provide specific examples. Next, they will describe what keeps this boundary in place.

As mental health providers, we have to realize that maladaptive patterns are in place for a reason; they serve a purpose in that they are reinforcing and they work – but with a high cost to clients and their well-being. Finally, clients will indicate if they can see themselves developing adaptive boundaries and describe what those adaptive boundaries would be like.

Use the next worksheet to help clients learn the characteristics and benefits of adaptive boundaries to help clients clarify in their minds their boundaries and the benefits. Be sure to prepare them for the "pushback" they are likely to receive when establishing new boundaries, but it is important to hold true to what is adaptive and healthy for them.

MY BOUNDARIES AND BEYOND

This activity is designed to help you identify what type of boundary you currently have with your partner who is along the narcissistic spectrum and help you develop more adaptive boundaries. Adaptive boundaries will help you have better control over your life and yourself, as well as to interact more authentically with those closest to you. There are four types of boundaries: Solid, Loose, Broken, and Adaptive.

Solid boundaries are those walls that are impenetrable and through which no one can get. Individuals with these boundaries shut out others and the world. They do not listen to or take suggestions from others, are unlikely to ask for help, are highly protective of personal information, and are likely to be detached from their romantic partners because they are seemingly content being alone in their own world. Individuals along the narcissistic spectrum often have these boundaries out of fear, shame, doubt, guilt and inferiority. Partners in relationships with individuals along the narcissistic spectrum are initially unlikely to have these boundaries, but they may eventually establish them when they have shut down or given up. In turn, they may use these boundaries to lock out the world to prevent further abuse or harm.

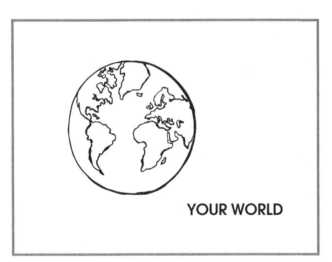

YOUR WORLD

Loose boundaries are those that are "see through," such that information, opinions, requests, and viewpoints of others come in without question because others are seen as having more knowledge and intellect. Individuals with these boundaries tend to provide too much personal information, have difficulty saying "no," are overinvolved with others, fear rejection if they do not comply, are dependent on other people's opinions, and are likely to accept abuse or disrespect.

Individuals along the narcissistic spectrum are unlikely to have this type of boundary, as it goes against their narcissistic defense mechanism to shield their fear, shame, doubt, guilt and inferiority. Partners in relationships with individuals along the narcissistic spectrum are likely to possess this type of boundary because their partner is seen as the gatekeeper of opinions, information, knowledge, and approval that they feel they themselves are lacking.

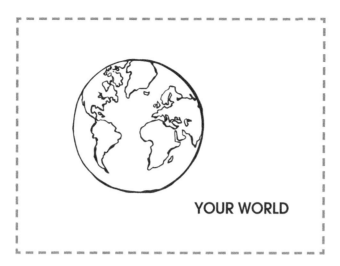

YOUR WORLD

Broken boundaries are those that were once strong and clear but have been fractured by pain and experience. These individuals tend to justify maltreatment, blame themselves when things go wrong, and have a high degree of self-doubt and shame. At the same time, though, they know something is off because they once had adaptive boundaries and a healthy sense of self. Individuals along the narcissistic spectrum are unlikely to have these boundaries because it requires insight into past negative experiences that are likely blocked out and do not support their distorted worldview.

Partners in relationships with individuals along the narcissistic spectrum are likely to have this type of boundary because being in a relationship with a narcissistic partner has eroded their sense of self, opinions, and view of the world.

YOUR WORLD

Adaptive boundaries are those that permit information, opinions, feelings, and reactions to be evaluated as appropriate and not harmful. These individuals value the opinions of others, do not inappropriately compromise who they are, appropriately share personal information, know what they want and need and express this properly, and will say and accept "no" from others when deemed necessary.

Individuals along the narcissistic spectrum and their partners are unlikely to have these boundaries because they require adaptive skills to evaluate others, themselves, and the world around them, and they do not tolerate the cyclical abuse often present in the relationship. However, when the partner of a narcissistic individual comes to treatment, it is a good sign that he or she may be ready to start building adaptive boundaries.

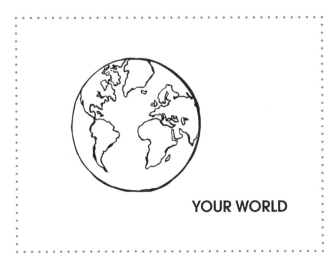

YOUR WORLD

Identify which boundary you feel you have in your relationship:

☐   Solid   ☐   Loose   ☐   Broken   ☐   Adaptive

Describe your boundary type using clear and specific examples:

_____

_____

_____

Describe what keeps your boundary in place:

_____

_____

_____

Can you see yourself having adaptive boundaries?

☐   YES   ☐   NO

Describe how you see yourself and your life if you developed adaptive boundaries:

_____

_____

_____

Developing adaptive boundaries takes time and patience. Visualizing adaptive boundaries and the positive influence they have on you and your life is critical to developing and maintaining a healthy self and having healthy relationships.

CONTENDING WITH GASLIGHTING

Gaslighting is a term from a 1944 movie called "Gaslight" where a husband tries to convince his wife that she is mentally ill by making small changes in her environment, such as turning down the gas lights and telling her they do not look turned down to him but only to her. This term has since become synonymous with abuse and manipulation, and it is often seen in relationships with individuals along the narcissistic spectrum.

Typically, gaslighting occurs when the partner of the individual along the narcissistic spectrum brings up an issue of concern, and the narcissistic individual (called "gaslighter" in the example below) turns the response on the partner so that it becomes the partner's fault. Over time, the partner begins to question his or her own beliefs, opinions, and values. For example:

Partner:	"Are you cheating on me?"
Gaslighter:	"How could I cheat on you?"
Partner:	"You're never home, you come home late, and you change your phone passcode once a week."
Gaslighter:	"I am working to give you the things you want; I work overtime to make more money for you, and I change my passcode weekly for safety because you misplace my phone every time you clean the house. Maybe if you tried harder, worked more, and cleaned up without moving my phone, things would be better, and you wouldn't be so paranoid."
Partner:	"You're right, I'll try harder."

Being the victim of gaslighting can have long-term effects, including second guessing oneself about things one knows to be true, isolation from family and friends, loss of honest and caring support, greater dependency on the abuser, fear of being seen as unstable or as a liar, or increased symptoms of anxiety, depression, paranoia, and other mental health disorders. Knowing what gaslighting is, identifying it, and helping your client overcome it is the purpose of this activity.

NEXT STEPS

Provide clients with the **Overcoming Gaslighting** activity. Go over the responses with them, and look for themes that may be present. Gaslighting is managed and countered by increasing awareness of and building skills to destroy it. Reinforce those responses that block or prevent gaslighting, and make sure to note the individuals mentioned in clients' support networks who can help. Support from others is a critical component to overcoming gaslighting, as these individuals are the ones to whom clients can go to get verification of their sanity and support for their beliefs.

OVERCOMING GASLIGHTING

Gaslighting is a tactic often used in relationships by individuals along the narcissistic spectrum to cause their partners to second-guess themselves and ultimately become uncertain of their thoughts, feelings, and views of the world. This activity will help you identify and overcome this abusive tactic.

Mark (√) all of the gaslighting tactics you experience in your relationship:

☐ Your partner refuses to listen to your concerns or pretends not to understand them.

☐ Your partner questions your memory of events and denies events the way you remember them.

☐ Your partner changes the topic or minimizes your concern on topics you know to be valid and accurate.

☐ Your partner tells you that you make up things that you know have taken place.

☐ Your partner often claims that you are overreacting even when you are slightly upset.

☐ You feel confused about how events occurred, even though you know they happened a particular way.

☐ You withhold information to avoid making excuses and having to explain something, though you feel sure of it on the inside.

☐ You feel like you cannot do anything right.

☐ You withhold information from friends and family out of fear of being seen as unstable or unbalanced.

☐ You defer to your partner for confirmation of facts to avoid the fear of being wrong or misunderstood.

Describe an instance when you were made to be unsure of something by your partner:

_____

_____

What was said that made you question the accuracy of the instance?

_____

_____

Circle how much you believe your recollection to be true on the scale below:

1	2	3	4	5
Totally Untrue	Sort of Untrue	Not Sure	Sort of True	Totally True

Support your belief with concrete details. These are details that even a stranger would agree with 100% (facts of the situation that are clear and verifiable): _____

_____

_____

When you feel uncertain in the future, which of the following statements will you feel comfortable using to confront gaslighting?

☐ "You're trying to tell me what my experience is, and I am entitled to my own viewpoint."

☐ "You are making me feel uncomfortable, and I want to take a break from talking right now."

☐ "We have to agree to disagree."

☐ "I have a right to what I believe, even if it's different from your belief."

What are some other things you can say to counter gaslighting in your relationship?

_____

_____

Make a list of people in your support network who have faith in and believe in you (your name goes first)**:**

_____

_____

POWER TO CHOOSE

Empowerment is a critical component when working with individuals in a relationship with someone along the narcissistic spectrum. Recognizing and utilizing the power to choose their response when triggered is critical to addressing and changing maladaptive patterns and to protect against being manipulated. The manipulation process tends to go in this sequence:

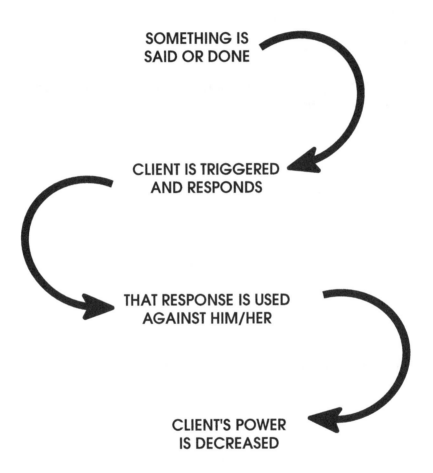

This sequence tends to occur multiple times throughout the relationship, and the end result is that clients lose their will to counter the response and just accept the abuse and belittling. Relationships with individuals along the narcissistic spectrum have an inherent component of making the partner feel less powerful, important, and valued. This devaluation provides individuals along the narcissistic spectrum with a false sense of control over the relationship, as they blame the partner for any failure or mistakes that occur. This exercise is designed to help clients feel more powerful in and have better control over these situations, as well as to teach them strategies that will prevent them from being manipulated or having their behavior used against them.

NEXT STEPS

The following exercise, called **Power to Choose**, will help clients recognize their triggers and clarify their responses. Having greater emotional control will provide a sense of empowerment for your client, and this is a critical component that was likely given away as the relationship progressed. Revisit this exercise multiple times, and be sure to pull out this exercise when clients are using these strategies and gaining greater control over themselves and their maladaptive patterns.

POWER TO CHOOSE

In many relationships with individuals along the narcissistic spectrum, any misstatement or immediate response is met with ridicule and devaluing. This exercise is designed to help you manage these instances by identifying your triggers (e.g., something occurs and you have an immediate response) and creating counter responses to give you better control over yourself and these situations. By doing this, you increase your personal power and control, and you can better manage yourself and the relationship.

Triggers can be people, places, things, thoughts, feelings, or situations. Triggers are as unique to each individual as is the response in which each person engages when triggered. Be as descriptive as you can when describing your triggers, and answer to the best of your ability. There are no right or wrong answers.

What are your triggers? _____

_____

_____

What triggers does your partner usually engage in that set you off?

_____

_____

What is your usual response when you get triggered? _____

_____

_____

How is your triggered behavior used against you? _____

_____

_____

Mark (√) which of the following strategies you can use the next time you are triggered (mark all that apply)**:**

☐ Remind yourself that you have the power to choose your response

☐ Leave the situation and walk it off

☐ Refuse to engage when you are angry

☐ Play a game on your phone after leaving the situation

☐ Remind yourself that your power is yours to keep or give away

☐ Relax your body, clear your thoughts, center your awareness on your body, and focus on a keyword that empowers you, like CHOICE

☐ Call a friend or someone you trust

☐ Eat or drink something that is opposite of the weather; for example, if it is hot outside, drink something cold

☐ Workout or exercise

☐ Imagine a time in your life when you felt safe and secure

☐ List 3 things in your life that are positive

☐ Act opposite to your negative feelings

☐ Reward yourself when you do not succumb to the trigger

☐ Pray, meditate, or use mindfulness (ask your mental health provider about this invaluable skill)

What do you gain by exercising the power to choose how you respond when you are triggered?

_____

_____

Digging Deeper into Motivations and Lessening Symptomatology

BECOMING DISCONNECTED FROM THE NARCISSIST

Those who are in relationships with individuals along the narcissistic spectrum are contending with the difficult issue of continuing or ending the relationship. What makes it so difficult is that it pertains to more than just the relationship, but also to how they see themselves and their sense of worth.

Your clients' sense of worth likely feels tethered and tied to the individual along the narcissistic spectrum. By ending the relationship, they are cutting their partner loose and becoming untethered and untied. Importantly, they are also losing a part of themselves, acknowledging a perceived failure, and confronting their fear of being alone, worthless, and unlovable forever, which feeds into their distorted self-view. Their inability to see themselves accurately has resulted in their continuing the relationship without exploration, without empowering themselves, and without recognition of choice. The recognition of choice is critical for partners in relationships with individuals along the narcissistic spectrum because choice provides the power to continue it or end it.

This next exercise is designed to help clients explore their relationship, build insight, examine the costs and benefits of continuing or ending the relationship, recognize what they get out of the relationship, and explore their ability to be self-sufficient without the relationship. This exercise will also teach them the importance of deciding to be in the relationship because they *want* to, not because they *have* to, as well as the steps to dissolve the relationship should they make that choice. Many mental health providers assume that clients know the steps to dissolve a relationship, but partners in relationships with individuals along the narcissistic spectrum may have little or no idea how to do this, and this is an important skill to learn, whether or not they make the choice to use it.

NEXT STEPS

The decision to continue or end the relationship is a difficult concept to address, and one that clients are likely to be afraid to explore and on which they will waver greatly. However, framing this exercise as one that is exploratory in nature lessens the responsibility of having to make a decision now and forever. This exercise is not a method to force your clients to decide but, rather, a means to help them explore their options and recognize the choices they have in the relationship.

Your clients can complete the **My Relationship, My Choice** worksheet in session, or you give it to them as homework, so they can explore their relationship. You want to be sure to revisit the responses on more than one occasion, as this is not a single use exercise. It may also need to be updated periodically as your client continues in the relationship or enters into new ones.

MY RELATIONSHIP, MY CHOICE

You have a powerful choice in front of you, though sometimes it is difficult to see that the choice is yours. However, the choice to continue or end any relationship *is* up to you. This exercise will help you through the steps to determine if your relationship is one that you want to continue or end and help you decide what is best for you. Be as honest and descriptive as you can, and go over the results with your therapist.

If you knew a friend or loved one was in a relationship similar to yours, would you want him/her to continue it?

☐   YES   ☐   NO

What is it about the relationship that you would want your friend to consider before ending it or continuing it? _____

_____

_____

What is more important in your relationship?

☐ My Partner's Feelings   ☐ My Feelings

Describe how it feels to have your partner's feelings or your feelings considered more important:

_____

_____

What would have to happen for you to continue the relationship?

_____

_____

What would have to happen for you to end the relationship? _____

_____

_____

When you think about continuing it, what comes to your mind?

_____

_____

When you think about ending it, what comes to your mind? _____

_____

_____

What do you get out of the relationship? _____

_____

_____

Can you give yourself the same things that you get out of the relationship?

☐   YES   ☐   NO

Describe how you could give yourself the things you get out of the relationship:

_____

_____

Steps to dissolving the relationship:

1. Make sure you, and your children (if applicable), have a safe place to go.

2. Create a plan to put physical distance between you and your ex-partner.

3. Allow yourself to feel the grief that everyone feels at the end of a relationship. This grief does not mean that you cannot live without your partner, and the stages of grief are not always chronological but can include movement back and forth and in different directions.

    a. **Denial** that it is over, and you want to go back.

    b. **Anger** that you were not treated better.

    c. **Bargaining** with your partner to make the relationship better so you can go back.

    d. **Depression/sadness** over the end of the relationship. This sadness does not mean that you need to go back; it means that you are sad over the loss of a relationship – whether that relationship was good or bad.

    e. **Acceptance** that the relationship is over, and you can move forward.

4. Find social support outside of your circle with your partner.

5. Continue in therapy to process and examine your feelings outside the relationship and learn how to build new, healthy relationships.

7 RELATIONSHIP HOPES AND REALITIES

Healthy relationships are characterized by the 7 Relationship Hopes and Realities, which include: Here-and-Now, Support, De-escalation, Consideration, Trust, Responsibility-taking, and Energy (see worksheets below for descriptions of each). All of us want to have these 7 Relationship Hopes and Realities in our relationships. However, individuals who have partners along the narcissistic spectrum are likely to have few or none of these, and this is sometimes what draws them into treatment.

The following exercise is designed to help clients see their relationship honestly by providing a description of the 7 Relationship Hopes and Realities on a continuum. For example, "Here-and-Now" is on one end, while "Lost in the Past" is on the other. This worksheet can help increase clients' understanding of their relationships and increase insight into where they may fall on the continuum.

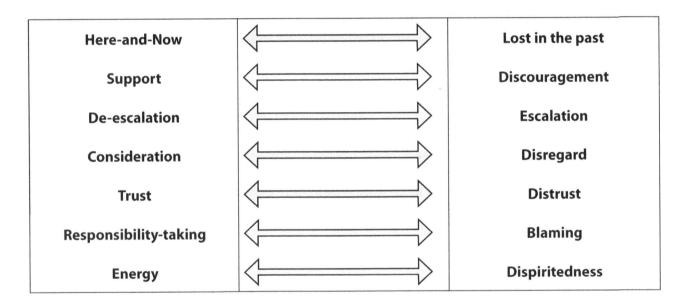

As mental health providers, our job is to help our clients recognize what is and is not in their relationship, and help them move in a direction of greater fulfillment. Our clients can choose healthier relationships, but they have to know the direction in which they are heading and what it will look like when they get there.

NEXT STEPS

This exercise can help your clients solidify what they want out of the relationship by teaching them to recognize what is actually in the relationships. A description of the **7 Relationship Hopes and Realities** is provided first, followed by a chart depicting these areas on a continuum. The second section of the exercise asks clients to describe at which end of the continuum their relationships fall. This information is critical to helping clients solidify what they want and to determine if their needs are being met in their relationship.

The final part of the exercise asks clients to describe or draw a picture of what their relationship would look like if the 7 Relationship Hopes and Realities were present. This exercise allows clients to visualize their relationship, which is a powerful experience for them, but it also helps the therapist use this information as therapy progresses to reinforce the picture of a healthy and satisfying relationship.

7 RELATIONSHIP HOPES AND REALITIES

Below are the 7 Relationship Hopes and Realities that make up healthy relationships. Each is described below to help you determine if these qualities are present in your relationship, followed by a continuum showing both ends of the 7 Relationship Hopes and Realities. The left side of the continuum lists the 7 Relationship Hopes and Realities, and the right side of the continuum lists the opposite of these qualities, which are the components that cause us to lose hope in our relationships, and sometimes in ourselves.

The second part of the exercise asks you to describe how each of the 7 Relationship Hopes and Realities, or their opposite, is present in your relationship. The last part asks you to write out or draw a picture of what your relationship would look like if the 7 Relationship Hopes and Realities were present. Use this information with your therapist to help you create that picture.

Here-and-Now	You are able to discuss and manage one issue at a time and what you need in the relationship without bringing up past wounds or blaming the other person for problems or lost hopes.
Support	You genuinely support each other and expressive yourselves through authentic emotional gestures when in distress. There is little to no "kicking you when you're down" or negativity when you are struggling.
De-escalation	You do not "go too far" with words or gestures to hurt the other person. Effort is applied to calm tense moments. There is little to no bringing up painful past experiences or statements, and you do not have a strong desire to verbally and mentally destroy the other.
Consideration	You and your partner pay attention to each other's feelings, thoughts, and values. There is little to no interrupting, talking over each other, dismissing, or minimizing, and your partner will stop negative behaviors when asked.
Trust	There is a foundational belief in each other's reliability, truth, ability, and strength. You do not undermine each other to prove your worth.
Responsibility-taking	The relationship is an open and safe environment where you can both admit to mistakes and take blame when it is due for obvious actions. You do not place sole blame on each other for problems in the relationship or "turn tables" so the other is completely at fault.
Energy	There is passion, vigor, spirit, and strength that are gained from being in the relationship. The relationship is not "soul sucking," and it does not drain you of your drive to succeed or your hopes for the future.

Here-and-Now	⟷	**Lost in the past**
Support	⟷	**Discouragement**
De-escalation	⟷	**Escalation**
Consideration	⟷	**Disregard**
Trust	⟷	**Distrust**
Responsibility-taking	⟷	**Blaming**
Energy	⟷	**Dispiritedness**

Describe how **Here-and-Now** or **Lost in the Past** is present in your relationship: _____

_____

_____

Describe how **Support** or **Discouragement** is present in your relationship: _____

_____

_____

Describe how **De-escalation** or **Escalation** is present in your relationship: _____

_____

_____

Describe how **Consideration** or **Disregard** is present in your relationship: _____

_____

_____

Describe how **Trust** or **Distrust** is present in your relationship: _____

_____

_____

Describe how **Responsibility-taking** or **Blaming** is present in your relationship: _____

_____

_____

Describe how **Energy** or **Dispiritedness** is present in your relationship: _____

_____

_____

THE PICTURE OF THE 7 RELATIONSHIP HOPES AND REALITIES

Use the space below to describe or draw a picture of what your relationship would look like if the 7 Relationship Hopes and Realities were present. You can do this in writing or as a drawing in the space below. As a reminder, the 7 Relationship Hopes and Realities are: Here-and-Now, Support, De-escalation, Consideration, Trust, Responsibility-taking, and Energy.

WANT, DESERVE, MUST HAVE

In many relationships with individuals along the narcissistic spectrum, partners lose sight of themselves and what they want, deserve, or must have in the relationship. The "want" refers to what clients aspire to have in the relationship, the "deserve" is what they feel entitled to in the relationship but may not be getting, and the "must-have" is the critical piece that keeps them in the relationship. For example, clients may "want" to have unconditional love, "deserve" for their partner to be patient with them, and "must have" a non-physically abusive relationship. The goal of this exercise is to help clients identify what gives them a sense of satisfaction and purpose in the relationship, as well as to clarify if these needs are being met by the relationship. Doing so will help clients to identify their motivations for staying and reduce symptoms that keep them in a relationship that is not providing them with what they want, deserve, or must have.

NEXT STEPS

After your client has completed the following Want, Deserve, Must Have worksheets, look for similarities in responses and themes that indicate underlying core needs that the client is trying to get met. Explore where these needs come from, how it makes sense that they are in the current relationship based upon past experiences, and what they can do to empower themselves to get what they want, deserve, and must have. This is an exercise that has many uses throughout the course of therapy and should be revisited or referenced as your client develops more adaptive and healthy relationship wants, deserves, and must-haves.

WANT, DESERVE, MUST HAVE

In relationships, we sometimes give up what we want and what we need so that our partner will stay with us, be the person we want him or her to be, or give us affection so we feel loved. In doing so, we lose our sense of want, deserve, and must have in our relationships. In turn, we end up feeling invisible because our self-worth erodes over time. This activity is designed to help you identify what you want, deserve, and must have in your relationship and to empower you to be visible in your relationship and in your life. Be as specific as you can when completing your list. Utilize your therapist to help you identify your want, deserve, and must-have relationship components.

Relationship want list – List the 5 things you *want* in your relationship

1. _____
2. _____
3. _____
4. _____
5. _____

Relationship deserve list – List the 5 things you *deserve* in your relationship

1. _____
2. _____
3. _____
4. _____
5. _____

Relationship must-have list – List the 5 things you *must have* in your relationship

1. _____
2. _____
3. _____
4. _____
5. _____

Describe any similarities or themes you noticed: _____

_____

_____

Describe specific steps in which you can engage to get what you want, deserve, and must have in your relationship. Be as specific as you can, and consult your therapist for help.

1. _____

2. _____

3. _____

4. _____

5. _____

NO MORE ROLLERCOASTER

Many individuals feel as if they are on an emotional roller coaster by being in a relationship with an individual along the narcissistic spectrum. When this emotional turmoil reaches a certain point, the partner begins to feel a significant level of dissonance, which is often what drives him or her into treatment. To better control the emotional rollercoaster, clients will need to learn critical skills that will allow them to gain greater emotional stability in the relationship, even if this emotional stability is contrary to what they are accustomed. For example, they may be familiar with emotional turmoil in the home in which they grew up or in their past relationships, and they may find a false sense of safety in chaos. This exercise is designed to build the skills that are necessary to increase emotional stability in the relationship and to challenge core concerns that your client may have about doing things differently.

NEXT STEPS

Go over the six skills in the first section of the **No More Rollercoaster** worksheets with your client, and then ask him or her to complete the second page of the activity. As you go through the results, look for similar themes so you can link skills together, as it is easier to master one or two skills instead of six. Use these results over the course of multiple sessions to allow for skill building to occur.

NO MORE ROLLERCOASTER

The skills listed below will help you gain emotional stability in your relationship and will help you feel like you are *not* on an emotional rollercoaster with your partner. Read each skill, and then describe how you can implement each one into your relationship and your life in the section that follows. Adding these skills into your life and your relationship will help you get off the emotional rollercoaster.

Define your boundaries

This refers to knowing and allowing what you are comfortable with. It is different from tolerating what you have learned to accept; it consists of only permitting what feels right in your relationship. This includes how you are treated verbally, physically, mentally, sexually, and emotionally.

Independence

This means that you are able to function and do things on your own. This does not mean that you must do *everything* on your own, but that you are not dependent on others to allow you to do something that is good for yourself. This also includes not allowing someone else to prohibit you from doing something adaptive and healthy.

Get what you deserve

This entails allowing what you feel is right for you in your life and your relationship. Seek out what you feel it is that you deserve in your relationship, such as respect, appreciation, and understanding. Knowing these things will help you develop a sense of self that deserves to be treated in a clear, calm, and stable manner, as opposed to being exposed to emotional chaos.

Have a voice

Use your voice to undo the emotional rollercoaster. This includes being able to speak up for yourself and to honestly and clearly communicate your relationship wants and needs.

Avoid the assumption

In many emotionally chaotic relationships, each partner often acts as though he or she is a mind reader. In particular, they often attempt to interpret their partner's behavior and make assumptions regarding their partner's thoughts or mood. However, what this actually does is contribute to the emotional rollercoaster. When you find yourself making assumptions, ask for clarity. If the response you get is unclear, use your voice and ask for clarification.

Follow through consistently

One of the best ways to control the emotional rollercoaster is to say what you do and do what you say. This removes the need for interpretation and guesswork that adds to emotional instability. If you say something, be sure to follow through. If you know you have a different timeline than your partner, be clear about what your timeline is so the ambiguity does not build, as this can lead to frustration and the start of the emotional rollercoaster.

Describe how you can define your boundaries: _____

_____

_____

Describe how you can create independence: _____

_____

_____

Describe how you can get what you deserve: _____

_____

_____

Describe how you can have a voice: _____

_____

_____

Describe how you can avoid the assumption: _____

_____

_____

Describe how you can follow through: _____

_____

_____

BUILDING ON THE FOUNDATIONAL 5

The Foundational 5 is made up of the critical components to sustaining a healthy relationship. It is composed of communication, mutual respect, trust, acceptance, and shared interests and values. Many relationships with individuals along the narcissistic spectrum lack many or all of these factors. Addressing these factors in therapy is helpful so that the partner of the individual along the narcissistic spectrum can make a conscious determination if these needs are being met. Adding clarity to the presence or absence of some, or all, of the Foundational 5 and how your client reacts will help build insight and define areas to work on, or it will clarify reasons for sustaining or dissolving the relationship.

The choice to sustain or dissolve the relationship is confusing and difficult for those in a relationship with an individual along the narcissistic spectrum. They often feel like they are going to lose a part of themselves if the relationship ends, but making the choice to remove pain or re-craft it into something positive (if possible) is an empowering experience that this activity can help your client make.

NEXT STEPS

Provide clients with the worksheets for **Building on the Foundational 5**, and go over the definitions for each of the Foundational 5 in session. Then, have clients fill out the remainder of the worksheets. The client can complete the worksheets in session or as homework, but be sure to go over the definitions in session so that you are certain that clients understand its components and what is being asked of them. If clients are unsure about what examples they can provide, work with them to identify examples; this is an excellent rapport building opportunity, as well as a chance to build insight into their relationships.

The second half of the worksheet provides building blocks for the Foundational 5 along with techniques to help build these skills. Help clients find one or two skills that they can implement. Ask them to circle which skills they would like to learn that would be the most helpful. Avoid cognitively overloading your clients by trying to implement too many skills at once. Skill building takes time and practice. You can rank order the Foundational 5 to help identify the most salient skills that need to be included in a client's relationship and the ones that will be the most helpful.

The last part of the activity is likely the most difficult. It instructs clients to look at their relationships and the components of the Foundational 5 from a global view and to then describe how they see their relationships. Many clients find this difficult because they know "on some level" that the relationship is problematic and that their partner, who is along the narcissistic spectrum, is resistant to the Foundational 5 or only wants the components that benefit him or her. This final activity can open up discussion about the longevity of the relationship and can help a client determine whether to continue it or end it (see Together or Apart worksheet in this workbook for more assistance in helping your client make this important decision).

BUILDING ON THE FOUNDATIONAL 5

The Foundational 5 is composed of communication, mutual respect, trust, acceptance, and shared interests and values. Relationships that lack reciprocity in terms of these five critical relationship components are more likely to have difficulties. When evaluating a relationship, we have to consider each component separately, then as a whole, to have the clearest perspective on the relationship and its overall health and impact.

This activity first asks you to identify examples of how each of the Foundational 5 are present or absent in your relationship. If the answer is "I don't know," that is all right, and you can discuss this with your therapist to find one. In the second section, there are three building blocks for each of the Foundational 5 components with techniques to help build these skills. Circle which technique you think would fit into your relationship, and then describe how you will implement it.

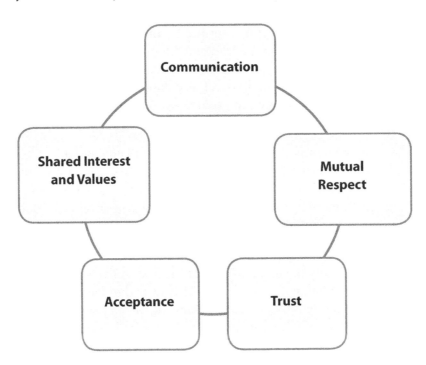

The first step is to define each of the Foundational 5:

Communication

Communication is both verbal and nonverbal, and includes speaking and behaving in an open and clear manner. When disagreements occur, both individuals work toward solutions without criticizing or disrespecting each other, and the messages they convey are coherent and understandable. When communication is poor in a relationship, messages and meanings are distorted, causing both individuals to fill in the gaps with "guesswork" and assumptions. This process continually wears down on communication until there is a complete loss of openness and individuals can no longer safely speak their minds and hearts.

An example of **communication** in my relationship is: _____

_____

_____

Mutual Respect

Mutual respect is the ability to value another individual for his or her unique qualities and to accept his or her dreams and wishes. It promotes thoughtfulness and consideration between partners. Having mutual respect for one another means not disrespecting the other person to his or her face or behind his or her back. When mutual respect is lost or eroding in the relationship, both individuals begin to build resentment and look for ways to attack the other person and make him or her feel small and unimportant.

An example of **mutual respect** in my relationship is: _____

_____

_____

Trust

Trust is a feeling that you can count on the other person during good times and bad, and you know that he or she will do his or her best to help whenever possible. A central component of trust is keeping your word and your partner keeping his or hers. When trust is lost or fractured, the relationship begins to feel like walking on broken glass; it is hard, dangerous, and cuts deep as both individuals question if his or her partner will be there in times of trouble or need, or during times of inconvenience.

An example of **trust** in my relationship is: _____

_____

_____

Acceptance

Acceptance is the understanding that no one is perfect and that both individuals in the relationship are accepted for who they are. It provides the freedom to be open and comfortable with yourself and with your partner. When partners do not feel accepted in the relationship, both individuals tend to find other areas to get that need met. They may seek this out in social gatherings or other romantic relationships to supplement the emptiness.

An example of **acceptance** in my relationship is: _____

_____

_____

Shared Interests and Values

Similar interests, goals, values, and beliefs are factors that help both partners feeling comfortable and settled in the relationship. Not every aspect of the relationship needs to be the same, but having some common areas is important. When there are no shared interests or values in a relationship, or one partner feigns interest to stay connected to the other, the relationship takes on a weight and a level of work that wears away at each individual until this sense of disinterest begins to surface in other areas. This can lead to partners spending more time apart from one another or the dissolution of the relationship.

An example of **shared interests and values** in my relationship is: _____

_____

_____

HOW TO BUILD THE FOUNDATIONAL 5 IN YOUR RELATIONSHIP

In the next section, there are three building blocks for each of the Foundational 5 components with a list of techniques to help build that skill. Circle which technique(s) you think would fit into your relationship and then describe how you will implement it. Circle as many as you feel are appropriate for your relationship.

3 Building Blocks of Communication

Listening	Being aware of my body	Being brief and clear
• Ask questions about what you are hearing. • Do not talk over. Talk with, and hear what is being said. • Take turns speaking so each person has time to listen. Avoid formulating your response while the other person is speaking.	• Stand facing the person speaking. • Keep your posture open; do not cross your arms or legs. • Stay relaxed, even when you are hearing something you do not like.	• Know the point of your message before you communicate it. • Be aware of the knowledge level on the topic you are discussing, and try to be as short and succinct as possible.

I can implement the _____ technique(s) by _____

_____

_____

_____

3 Building Blocks of Mutual Respect

Showing genuine concern	Being helpful without having to be asked	Giving feedback instead of critiques
• Work to remember details about your partner's day and ask him/her about them. • Say your feelings slowly and with sincerity. • Do little things so your partner knows you are thinking about him/her in a positive way.	• If you see or know of something that would be helpful to your partner, just go ahead and do it. • If you notice that your assistance would be helpful, go ahead without waiting to see what happens next.	• Use "I" messages; say "I would have liked to..." • Sandwich difficult feedback between more forgiving feedback. Say something light, provide the feedback, then something light. That something light is best if positive.

I can implement the _____ technique(s) by _____

_____

_____

3 Building Blocks of Trust

Being reliable	Transparency	Valuing honor
• Be clear in your motives and intent, and follow through. If you cannot, be sure to tell the other person as soon as possible and explain why. • Be consistent, and act in a predictble manner when asked to do something or when handling an important matter.	• Be upfront and honest about how you feel. Make sure your verbal and nonverbal behaviors match. • Say "no" when you mean it and cannot do something. • Be sure to tell your partner what they need to know, and do not leave out details that may hurt him/her. A lie by omission can be more painful.	• Keep secrets secret, and avoid spreading gossip. • Show you are loyal to those around you; don't disparage others when they are not present. • Respect your feelings and the feelings of others by straightforwardly telling them, "I respect your feelings about that."

I can implement the _____ technique(s) by _____

_____

_____

3 Building Blocks of Acceptance

Open to self and others	Empathy	Win-win and win-lose scenarios
• You are willing to show weakness and strength while also receiving it from your partner. • When you see another person hurting, you recognize the humanness in the pain from the situation and do not attribute it to a failure of character. • Notice the sameness or difference in where you are in your life and your partner's, and embrace it without criticism.	• Picture in your mind what it is truly like to be that other person. Say to yourself, "If I were in his/her situation, I could understand." • Be a Radical Listener: listening with an "and" and not a "but," and trust others to be the best solvers of their own problems. Have faith in your partner's ability to develop ideas and implement solutions.	• Be open to allowing yourself to win along with your partner, but also be okay if s/he "wins" and you "lose." You may lose in the short-term and win a healthier relationship in the long-term. • Allowing your partner to win and you to lose builds the relationship, but it has to go both ways. One side cannot always win and one side always lose.

I can implement the _____ technique(s) by _____

_____

3 Building Blocks of Shared Interests and Values

Finding common interests	Sharing meaning	Differences create growth
• Look for small common interests upon which to build, such as foods, movies, places to go, dreams, etc. • Do something you both know nothing or very little about. Learn together and cultivate a common interest, such as cooking, learning a language, going to a store you would normally not go to, etc. • Find a common guilty pleasure and indulge together, such as chocolate, ice cream, TV shows, etc.	• Find common ground in how you define your relationship and what is important. • Help one another pursue dreams each had before the relationship began, and write out steps to help the other get there (your therapist can help here).	• Be open to what your partner likes, and never criticize him/her for the interest. • Discuss differences as a means to build a bridge to connect. Ask about the different interest, be open to learning about it, and value his/her choice to pursue the interest. • If each of you values the other's different interests, then that becomes a shared interest.

I can implement the _____ technique(s) by _____

_____

_____

When I look at the Foundational 5 and my relationship, I: _____

_____

_____

Final Steps

STAYING TOGETHER OR MOVING APART

Making a decision to continue a relationship or move away from it is never easy. This decision is often more complicated for those in relationships with individuals along the narcissistic spectrum because they tend to be in relationships that were or are initially exciting, rewarding, interesting, and supportive. However, the relationship eventually changed to only benefit the individual along the narcissistic spectrum, causing the partner to feel confused, lost, and uncertain, while still holding onto the thoughts, memories, and feelings of when the relationship began.

NEXT STEPS

This next exercise will challenge clients to examine their relationships by having them consider why they are in the relationships and why they would leave them. The first part of the exercise asks clients to list reasons for staying in or leaving the relationships. Next, they are asked to mark a box indicating which list is longer: the list for staying or leaving. This activity consists of a behavioral component (marking the box) and a visual component (seeing which box is marked) to help clients develop a clearer picture of which option has greater weight.

The next section asks clients to list the short-term and long-term impacts of staying in or leaving the relationships based upon which box is checked above, followed by another box for them to check which has the greatest impact. The last question is the most difficult and will require you (the mental health provider) to help clients weigh the valuable information derived from this exercise, the workbook, and the information and skills they have learned throughout therapy.

STAYING TOGETHER OR MOVING APART

This exercise is designed to help you make a clear and conscious decision to stay in the relationship or move away and end it. Use the spaces provided below to write out your reasons to stay in or leave the relationship. There are 10 spaces provided, but you can use the back of this sheet if you have more. Mark (√) the appropriate box to indicate if you have more reasons to stay in or leave the relationship.

After you have identified your reasons for staying or leaving, write out the short-term and long-term impact of maintaining or dissolving the relationship based upon which box you checked. Consider your feelings, thoughts, hopes, dreams, and the impact that staying or leaving has on others (e.g., children, parents) and on different settings (e.g., employment, social). Mark (√) the appropriate box to indicate if you have more short-term or long-term factors related to maintaining or dissolving the relationship. Discuss your responses with your therapist before answering the last question to help you arrive at a conclusion that is best for you.

I stay in the relationship because:

1. _____
2. _____
3. _____
4. _____
5. _____
6. _____
7. _____
8. _____
9. _____
10. _____

I would leave the relationship because:

1. _____
2. _____
3. _____
4. _____
5. _____
6. _____

7. _____

8. _____

9. _____

10. _____

I have more reasons to ☐ **stay** or ☐ **leave** the relationship.

Short-term impact of maintaining or dissolving the relationship would be:

1. _____

2. _____

3. _____

4. _____

5. _____

6. _____

7. _____

8. _____

9. _____

10. _____

Long-term impact of maintaining or dissolving the relationship would be:

1. _____

2. _____

3. _____

4. _____

5. _____

6. _____

7. _____

8. _____

9. _____

10. _____

The greatest impact will be in the ☐ **short-term** or ☐ **long-term**.

At this time, I am going to ☐ stay or ☐ leave the relationship.

UNDERSTANDING MYSELF AND MY RELATIONSHIP

As your clients have moved through the therapy process, they have developed knowledge, skills, and abilities to evaluate themselves, their partners, their relationships, and what they want out of their present and future relationships. This exercise is designed to help you and your clients identify areas of growth and understanding, so they can actually see in which areas they have made positive growth and in which areas they still need to focus.

While this activity is intended to provide a metric of where your clients are at the end of treatment, you can also use it as a pre- and post-treatment measure or at any point during the treatment process in order to provide insight into clients' growth and development. The statements in the activity examine key components related to clients' issues with codependency and their need to self-sacrifice what is of benefit to them for the betterment of their partners. This topic has likely been continually addressed throughout the course of treatment, and adding this exercise at the end of treatment (or any point in the process) helps build insight into areas where your clients have grown, issues they still need to be aware of, and/or what the focus of treatment should be going forward.

NEXT STEPS

Provide clients with the **Relationship and Self-Understanding Scale**, and ask them to complete it as best they can. The Relationship and Self-Understanding Scale can either be completed by you (the mental health provider) from the perspective of your client or by clients themselves. In some cases, both you and your clients can take the measure together to see if you agree on the results. Use the scale below to determine where clients fall on the continuum between relationship dependence or independence. Once you have the results, you can discuss the gains made in treatment, areas on which to focus in treatment (depending upon when in the process you administered this measure), and/or areas clients should be aware of going forward on their own.

Relationship and Self-Understanding Scale				
0-10	11-20	21-30	31-40	41-50
Dependent				Independent

RELATIONSHIP AND SELF-UNDERSTANDING SCALE

Please circle the number related to each statement that best represents your beliefs, thoughts, and perceptions of yourself, your partner, and your relationship. Answer all questions as honestly as you can. Once completed, return this questionnaire to your therapist to explore your results.

1. I have difficulty communicating my wants and needs in my romantic relationship.

①	②	③	④	⑤
Strongly Agree	Agree	Unsure	Disagree	Strongly Disagree

2. I value the approval of my partner more than I value myself.

①	②	③	④	⑤
Strongly Agree	Agree	Unsure	Disagree	Strongly Disagree

3. I do not trust myself to make decisions.

①	②	③	④	⑤
Strongly Agree	Agree	Unsure	Disagree	Strongly Disagree

4. I have fears that my partner will leave me and I will be all alone.

①	②	③	④	⑤
Strongly Agree	Agree	Unsure	Disagree	Strongly Disagree

5. I feel like I need my partner's approval before I make a decision or do anything.

①	②	③	④	⑤
Strongly Agree	Agree	Unsure	Disagree	Strongly Disagree

6. I would sacrifice my needs and the needs of those closest to me (i.e., children, family, etc.) for my partner.

①	②	③	④	⑤
Strongly Agree	Agree	Unsure	Disagree	Strongly Disagree

7. I feel responsible for the actions of others.

①	②	③	④	⑤
Strongly Agree	Agree	Unsure	Disagree	Strongly Disagree

8. It is hard for me to make decisions on my own when I am in a relationship.

①	②	③	④	⑤
Strongly Agree	Agree	Unsure	Disagree	Strongly Disagree

9. It is hard for me to identify my own feelings without considering how my partner interprets them.

①	②	③	④	⑤
Strongly Agree	Agree	Unsure	Disagree	Strongly Disagree

10. It is difficult for me to say "no" to my partner out of fear that he or she will become angry and/or leave me.

①	②	③	④	⑤
Strongly Agree	Agree	Unsure	Disagree	Strongly Disagree

Section 3

Treating **The Impact** of *Narcissistic Parents*

Setting the Stage for Successful Treatment

NARCISSISTIC FAMILY CHARACTERISTICS

The narcissistic family has many unique factors that are derived from the familial view that responsibility for emotional needs rests with the child or children, instead of with the parents, where it belongs (Donald-Pressman & Pressman, 1994; McBride, 2008). These include family secrets, abandonment anxiety, idealization of the child, fractured trust, emotional compliance, triangulation, misdirected communication, indistinct boundaries, and superficiality. These developmental distortions cause individuals who grew up in this type of family system to exhibit concerns and issues within most or all of their adult relationships. Children who grew up within this system form an unhealthy global perspective that influences how they see the world, interact with it, and develop relationships with significant others, friends, coworkers, and their own children.

Narcissistic family characteristics are more common than many mental health providers realize, and the impact of this type of family system tends to create a lifelong struggle for many clients who want to grow beyond their childhood experiences and make changes to their own lives and relationships. Increasing insight into narcissistic family characteristics increases the probability of success and influences long-term change in those clients who continue to fall into and recreate those early patterns in their adult lives.

This activity is designed to help increase that insight and assist clients in examining their lives and relationships, as well as their feelings and thoughts about changing and overcoming those characteristics. By doing so, they can start out on new adaptive and healthy pathways without the bonds of narcissistic family pathology.

NEXT STEPS

Provide clients with the **Narcissistic Family Characteristics** activity, and ask them to go through and place a mark (√) by the characteristics that match their family of origin. Once this is complete, clients will write out how these characteristics specifically apply to their families in order to increase insight and help them explore this issue in greater detail. As the mental health provider, it is important that you make clients aware of the likelihood that they will feel betrayal, anger, fear, confusion, etc. associated with addressing these issues. Narcissistic family characteristics are well-protected by the individual and the family, and the mental health provider must be able to address and discuss these issues, as they are likely to come up in the form of resistance.

NARCISSISTIC FAMILY CHARACTERISTICS

This activity will help you identify the narcissistic family characteristics related to your family of origin. Your family of origin does not have to be your biological family; it simply relates to the family in which you grew up. Place a mark (√) by each narcissistic family characteristic that corresponds with your family of origin.

Next, provide some examples to describe how the characteristics you have marked apply to your family system. It is important to remember that by doing this activity, you are not betraying any family trust; rather, you are seeking help to do things differently.

Engaging in this process will empower you and help you to overcome the psychological burden of growing up in this family system, and it will help you develop healthier and more adaptive functioning.

☐	**Family Secrets**	Emotional abuse and neglect are kept secret from those outside the family system to promote the "perfection" exterior. The children tend to be emotionally isolated from each other so there is no disruption of the "perfect" image. Children raised in this type of family system tend to have few memories growing up, and the ones that they have are vague and scattered.
☐	**Abandonment Anxiety**	Anxiety is prominent, and each child tries intensely to get attention and approval in order to maintain the "perfect" family image. Doing so maintains order and the status quo. Failure to maintain this image or to question it causes emotional banishment and stress. Children raised in this type of family system tend to have prominent psychological concerns related to anxiety and fear of abandonment.
☐	**Idealized Child**	One child is seen as the idealized child who does everything well, succeeds at everything (even minor attainments are highly praised as they prove the excellent job the parents are doing), and reaps the rewards of emotional caring and attention. Children from this family system, when not idealized, struggle with inferiority issues, second-guessing, and a vague internal pain of unmet needs.
☐	**Fractured Trust**	The system is inconsistent in providing emotional and physical support and, in turn, children learn that the system is unreliable and cannot be trusted in getting their needs met. Parents are cold and unaffectionate or they provide care and attention as they see fit (i.e., "When mom/dad feel like it"), as opposed to when the child needs it. Children from this family system approach others cautiously and with an underlying fear of being betrayed, ignored, and ultimately isolated because they are unable to emotionally trust another person.

☐	**Emotional Compliance**	Children learn to believe that they do not have a right to have or express feelings or thoughts that their parents or the family system deem unacceptable. They learn to "stuff it inward" or disregard their own feelings so that they do not upset the family system or cause problems for their parents. Children from this system tend to minimize or dismiss their own feelings and look to others for emotional confirmation and approval before acknowledging their own feelings.
☐	**Triangulation**	In trying to communicate with another person in the family system, the child pulls in someone else to convey the message (a third person – mom, dad, brother, sister, etc.), which creates a communication triangle and usually causes further confusion and tension in the process. Children from this system tend to unnecessarily involve others in order to be heard. Triangulation tends to minimize the power and influence of the message, causing feelings of uncertainty, low self-esteem, and powerlessness.
☐	**Misdirected Communication**	Messages are sent indirectly, resulting in confusion and passive-aggressive responses to perceived slights or insults. Children from this system tend to be highly anxious, second-guess direct messages, and communicate in an indirect fashion out of fear of being hurt.
☐	**Indistinct Boundaries**	Children have little to no emotional or physical privacy, cannot establish areas of their own, and are subject to their parents accessing their personal space at any time, including bedroom, bathroom, emails, phone calls, etc. Children from this system do not learn to set appropriate boundaries for themselves and have great difficulty saying "no."
☐	**Superficiality**	Children report feelings of having "thin" or superficial relationships with their parents. They do not experience a true emotional connection, and there is a lack of open and honest communication. Most communication is accomplished through unsolicited advice giving, demands, or denial of feelings because parents are focused elsewhere or "too busy" to address concerns. Children from this system tend to feel inferior and as if their needs are secondary to those of all or most other people. They value themselves very little.

Describe which characteristics match your family of origin and provide examples of each:

_____

_____

_____

_____

_____

Describe how these characteristics have affected your life and current relationships with significant others, friends, coworkers, and your own children: _____

_____

_____

_____

_____

_____

Describe your feelings and thoughts, without editing them, about overcoming your experiences with these family characteristics and starting out on a healthier path:

_____

_____

_____

_____

_____

COMPONENTS OF ADULT CHILDREN OF NARCISSISTS

Children who grew up being "cared for" by parents or caregivers along the narcissistic spectrum tend to develop psychological components that they carry with them all their lives. These components tend to become core structural components of how clients see the world, others, situations, and themselves. Many adult children of parents or caregivers along the narcissistic spectrum would not say that their home environment was overtly abusive. Rather, they typically described it as "That's just how it was [is]. That's just my mom [or dad]." The view that their home environments were harmful, undermining, or pathological is foreign to them because there may not have been physical or sexual abuse, so it is difficult for them to understand how there could be scars. However, parents or caregivers along the narcissistic spectrum cause psychological damage by wearing away at various points of psychological development that impact adaptive and healthy living. This activity is designed to build insight into the components of adult children of parents or caregivers along the narcissistic spectrum and to challenge and lessen the impact they have had on clients' lives.

NEXT STEPS

Provide your client with the **Components of Adult Children of Narcissists** activity. Be aware that many children of parents or caregivers along the narcissistic spectrum have a hard time objectively assessing impairment and functioning regarding themselves and others. Look for inconsistent responses, including what is and is not marked. Use these results as discussion points in sessions. The last part of the activity will help clients understand which components have the greatest impact on their lives today (and how), what areas of their lives are impacted the most (e.g., relationships, employment, etc.), and what about these components hold them back (e.g., "*Self-blame* makes things easier for everyone, so I just take the blame to make my parent or caregiver happy."). As an additional activity, you, the mental health provider, can complete the activity "through the eyes of your client" and compare and contrast the results to see how and why each of you see various components the same or differently.

Use this activity to help clients build insight into the challenges they need to overcome in order to start on healthier paths of functioning. This activity, in conjunction with the **Family of My Dreams** exercises, can be combined into a packet to help clients address and move past their family of origin issues

COMPONENTS OF ADULT CHILDREN OF NARCISSISTS

This list is made up of common components that many individuals experience having grown up with a parent or caregiver along the narcissistic spectrum. Mark (√) any components that correspond with how you see the world, yourself, and others, as well as how you feel about yourself. Once you have identified those components, fill out the statements below, and use this information in treatment to help you work through the components that are holding you back. By doing so, you can overcome your childhood experiences and start out on a new and healthier path free from the bonds of narcissistic family pathology.

☐	**Self-sacrifice**	The needs of your parents and others are more important than your own, so you sacrifice your own autonomy and independence to cater to others.
☐	**Self-blame**	You tend to sacrifice your self-esteem and blame yourself when things go wrong to keep things quiet and peaceful. You did this growing up to "keep the peace" or to please your parent/caregiver.
☐	**Buried under guilt**	Guilt was a tactic often used to get you to comply with your parent/caregiver while growing up. You tend to feel obligated to others as though you owe them something, including your complete obedience.
☐	**Compulsive caretaker**	To lessen the anxiety you feel associated with your own needs, you push them aside to take care of others. When problems arise, you do not trust your instincts, and you reach out to and seek continual reassurance from others.
☐	**Conditional approval**	When you make a mistake, you expect love to be withdrawn quickly and to receive rapid and intense punishment or to be dismissed altogether. When you do something to help someone and they reap a reward, you may then get the love you want and need. This cycle played out with your parent/caregiver and now with all others.

☐	**Perceived perfection**	You must present a veneer of love, success, and happiness at all times. Everything must seem perfect. Any flaws or errors are hidden and cause intense anxiety if people know they exist.
☐	**Your mistakes and your consequences**	Mistakes will cause others to see you as broken and unworthy. Your parent/caregiver never made a mistake and never apologized for an error, and when they did occur, you were often blamed for it. Now, you expect to be blamed and receive the consequences for even minor mistakes that may or may not involve you.
☐	**Gratitude giver**	You built your life as a means of showing your parent/caregiver how grateful you are and to build their self-esteem and worth. Any act of self-care is felt like a selfish betrayal and causes intense anxiety, unless you can identify someone else to reap the reward or gratitude.
☐	**Internalized narcissism**	You never get what you deserve, others have it easier, and others do not understand or appreciate your situation and experiences. You learned narcissism from your parent/caregiver, and you saw that it worked, so you used these tactics growing up and continue to use them in your current relationships.
☐	**Winner/loser**	You (or another family member) can do no wrong in your parent/caregiver's eyes, while the other family member (or you) can do nothing right and is riddled with ineptitude. You feel like you deserve certain things to work out and reap rewards or you feel guilty about success and prefer others to succeed.
☐	**Need to be needed**	You need to be needed by others to have a sense of worth. Your parent/caregiver tended to minimize your needs and intensify his/her own. You are most comfortable in relationships where you give and give, and appreciation or reciprocation cause anxiety and disinterest.
☐	**Emotional minimization**	You tend to minimize your own feelings, thoughts, opinions, and values because growing up these were not seen as valuable or were dismissed.

☐	**Competition is dirty**	Competing opens you up to ridicule and pain, and winning is very uncomfortable and feels wrong. Growing up, your parent/caregiver competed with you, and if you won, s/he would quit, become upset, ignore you, humiliate you, or a dole out a wide variety of other unwarranted negative consequences or punishments. You learned to feel that competition is unhealthy and can harm you, as opposed to driving you to do better.
☐	**Diffuse boundaries**	You are uncomfortable setting and holding firm with your boundaries. Growing up, your parent/caregiver dismissed your right to privacy in your own space. You learned that you were not valued enough to have your own space. In turn, you feel uneasy asserting your wants and needs, and are uncomfortable telling others what you will and will not tolerate.

Which components impact you the most today? _____

_____

_____

How do these components impact you today? _____

_____

_____

In what areas of your life do these components impact you the most (e.g., work, marriage, etc.)**?**

_____

_____

What about these components holds you back? _____

_____

_____

THE FAMILY OF MY DREAMS

Many children of parents or caregivers along the narcissistic spectrum develop fantasies of the perfect family that they will have when they grow up. They are driven by the idea that they will do it differently, treat their spouse and children with love and respect, and get it in return. The reality is that without the foundation of experience, they require skill building and insight to do things differently. Due to a distorted foundation, they typically end up trapped, reliving past pathology, and pick partners who manifest traits they understood as a child. This distortion becomes a part of their core structure (see Identifying Surface and Core Structures of Narcissistic Personality Disorder for more information on surface and core structures of personality).

The dream of the perfect family is a great motivator for clients who are children of parents or caregivers along the narcissistic spectrum. It is an intrinsic need that they have, and this can serve as a powerful force to help them move from the dynamics of their narcissistic families of origin to a healthy approach with themselves and their families. This exercise is designed to help them tap into that motivation and build the skills needed to learn the difference between their families then, now, and in the future; what is preventing them from achieving the family dream; and asking them to clarify steps to achieve it.

NEXT STEPS

Provide clients with **The Family of My Dreams** worksheet in session or as homework. Once completed, examine their responses and look for themes in the keywords associated with their families of origin, current families, and dream families. Are these themes hopeful, dysphoric, fearful, and/or regretful?

Themes provide an abundance of information and tell us so much, so it is important to process these themes in session and look for them in other areas of clients' lives. In addition, assess the descriptions that clients have written for differences between their past/current/dream families, barriers against moving forward, and the concrete steps they can take to create the family experience that they really want. The last question should be operationally defined to the greatest extent possible. The more concrete the steps are, the better you are able to gauge clients' progress toward reaching their dream family goals. This exercise can be revisited on multiple occasions throughout the therapy process to help maintain clients' motivation to change.

THE FAMILY OF MY DREAMS

Dreams are critical to helping us move forward and defining what we want out of life. Many individuals who are children of parents or caregivers along the narcissistic spectrum have dreams of a family that is filled with love, understanding, mutual respect, and guidance. However, these dreams are often in conflict with the family in which they grew up and the family in which they are now. To achieve our dreams, we need them to be well defined; otherwise, it makes it difficult to create them in the first place. To best define our dreams, we have to take the steps necessary to put the pieces together. This exercise will help you put together those pieces, identify the family of your dreams, and figure out how to get there.

Family that was, that is, and will be:

Describe the family in which you grew up using 5 to 8 keywords:

Describe your current family using 5 to 8 keywords:

Describe your dream family using 5 to 8 keywords:

Describe differences between the family in which you grew up, your current family, and your dream family: _____

_____

_____

What prevents you from creating your dream family today? _____
_____

_____

What steps can you take to create your dream family today? Be as specific as possible:

_____

_____

Addressing and Changing Maladaptive Patterns

AVOIDING "THE FAMILY CRUCIBLE" TRAP

The roles within families that include parents or caregivers along the narcissistic spectrum tend to be very similar to those roles seen in families with substance abuse. In order to address and change maladaptive patterns, clients must be aware of the roles into which they tend to fall when interacting with their parent or caregiver along the narcissistic spectrum. Enhancing this awareness and challenging clients to see its impact, its purpose, and how to avoid it, as well as defining aspirational goals, will help clients move forward from the effects of narcissistic pathology and allow them to develop a healthier view of themselves, others, and the world.

NEXT STEPS

Provide your client with the **Avoiding "The Family Crucible" Trap** activity in session or as homework. Examine the roles that clients marked as those in which they engage most often and the reasons for which they do so. Unhealthy roles are used for a reason, and identifying these reasons can be illuminating for both the mental health provider and the client. It is important to subsequently identify steps that clients can take in order to avoid falling into these usual role(s) and to write these steps down so clients are provided with a concrete plan and have a greater sense of empowerment and control over situations.

Most clients are going to pick "The Healthy" role as the role in which they would like to be, which can provide them with an aspirational goal toward which to work in treatment. Ask clients to describe what being in "The Healthy" role would be like, what it would mean, and what they would have to do in order to get into that role and stay there.

This activity can be used multiple times to assess if clients are falling into different roles as they grow and move toward healthier and more adaptive role representations.

AVOIDING "THE FAMILY CRUCIBLE" TRAP

Below is a chart with the most common roles into which individuals fall when growing up with a parent or caregiver along the narcissistic spectrum. The final role, "The Healthy" role, is not typically seen in individuals who grew up with a parent or caregiver along the narcissistic spectrum, but it is listed as something to which you can aspire. This role is a healthy role representation that is achievable.

This activity is designed to help you identify the role(s) into which you fall most often with your family, help you determine why, and help you determine what you can do to avoid it. It will also help you identify the role into which you would like to fall and why. This activity is the first step to address and change the impact that your family role has had on you.

The Family Crucible	This individual is the "guilt receptacle" and "problem child." All of the family's contempt for each other, failures, and problems with imperfection are put onto this individual. S/he is the family scapegoat and feels rejected, guilty, jealous, and angry inside.
The Avoider	This individual has shutdown from the chaos and abuse within the family. S/he has developed a coping strategy of avoidance when stress occurs and when in threatening situations. S/he has given up and feels empty, alone, afraid, depressed, and uncertain about his/her life.
The Hero	This individual does things to draw attention to him/herself in order to take the negative consequences away from others. S/he is inclined to take care of others and excel to help the parent or caregiver look and feel good. S/he feels guilty, hurt, and insecure about who s/he is and the pain that others are experiencing.
The Enabler	This individual maintains the status quo within the narcissistic family structure by encouraging and pacifying negative behavior. S/he will do anything to avoid the parent or caregiver becoming upset or hurt owing to their narcissistic views and parenting style. S/he feels angry, hurt, guilty, and insecure about his/her life choices and inability to satisfy everyone all the time.
The Rebel	This individual is prone to anger and acting out. S/he pushes things to the extreme and may self-sabotage in order to hurt the parent or caregiver and show his/her contempt. S/he feels angry, resentful, and afraid about the future and about the unpredictable way family members treat him/her.
The Mascot	This individual falls in line with the narcissistic pathology, does not cause problems, and will try to be pleasant all the time. S/he tries to be the "family favorite" to control internal fear, anxiety, and insecurity.

The Healthy	This individual is able to assert him/herself appropriately and receives an appropriate amount of love and attention. S/he is challenged to grow into an independent and thoughtful individual. S/he feels secure, confident, happy, and thankful for life and the people in it.

Which role(s) do you fall into most with your family and why? _____

_____

_____

What does falling into this role with your family do for you? _____

_____

_____

What can you do to avoid falling into that unwanted role? _____

_____

_____

What role would you like to be in with your family and why? _____

_____

_____

SELF-DEFINITION BEYOND NARCISSISTIC PARENTING PATHOLOGY

Many individuals who grew up with parents or caregivers along the narcissistic spectrum tend to have an unclear and negative view of themselves. Typically, parents or caregivers were not focused on helping these children define themselves, their worlds, and those around them. This is a distorted process that tends to create maladaptive patterns that hinder your client's functioning. This activity is designed to challenge clients to define who they are and how they see themselves, the world, and others. This is not an easy exercise for these individuals; clients will likely require a lot of encouragement and support, but it can help create achievable goals and move them toward functioning in a healthier and more adaptive manner.

NEXT STEPS

Go over the different parts of the **Defining a New Sense of Self** worksheet because it is likely to have many aspects that your client has not considered as a result of growing up with a parent or caregiver along the narcissistic spectrum. You can provide clients with this worksheet in session or as homework. Once it is complete, ask them to read their answers to you; this provides a deeper sense of realism and understanding of the answers provided. As clients are reading their answers, listen for themes related to how they see themselves, others, and the world. This exercise can be used multiple times throughout the course of treatment and to help create treatment goals.

DEFINING A NEW SENSE OF SELF

How we define ourselves is as important as how we think, behave, and act. The definition that we have of ourselves tends to be derived from our experiences and how we were treated growing up. Individuals who grew up with parents or caregivers along the narcissistic spectrum tend to have an uncertain or negative definition of themselves. This worksheet is designed to help you identify what comprises your current definition and to encourage you to explore redefining yourself and how you want others to see you.

DEFINE YOUR IDENTITY

Describe who you are because of your past: _____

_____

_____

Describe who you will be because of your choice to do things differently:

_____

_____

Describe your attitude because of your past: _____

_____

_____

Describe your attitude because of your choice to do things differently:

_____

_____

Describe your beliefs because of your past: _____

_____

_____

Describe your beliefs because of your choice to do things differently:

_____

_____

Describe your relationships because of your past: _____

_____

_____

Describe your relationships because of your choice to do things differently:

_____

_____

DEFINE YOUR VALUES

What traits or characteristics do you value the most about yourself?

_____

_____

What traits or characteristics would you like to have that you value in others?

_____

_____

What activities or accomplishments do you value the most? _____

_____

_____

What activities or accomplishments would you like to do more often?

_____

_____

IDENTIFY YOUR ACCOMPLISHMENTS AND CHALLENGES

What are your proudest accomplishments? _____

_____

_____

What is the impact of these accomplishments on how you think and feel about yourself?

_____

_____

What are your greatest challenges? _____

_____

_____

How have you managed these challenges? _____

_____

_____

What could you do, or continue to do, to lessen these challenges in the future?

_____

_____

DESCRIBE YOUR NEWLY DEFINED SELF

What is your new purpose and what has great meaning for you going forward?

_____

_____

What do you want to accomplish in the future? _____

_____

_____

What can you do to achieve your accomplishments in the future?

_____

_____

Identify 5 words you would like other people to use to describe you 5 years from now:

What can you do to encourage others to see you this way in the future?

_____

_____

A DUCK IN THE RAIN

Individuals who grew up in homes with parents or caregivers along the narcissistic spectrum had to contend with backhanded and double-edged comments. These comments can sound positive and encouraging on the surface, but because the child/client knows what the parent or caregiver really intends, the hurtful translation is clear. These comments work in favor of the parents or caregivers along the narcissistic spectrum because when the child/client tells others what was said, they claim that the child/client is being too sensitive and misinterpreted the comment. In turn, the parent or caregiver is seen as encouraging, and the child/client is faulted for the misinterpretation, which minimizes the reality of the hurt and pain. The goal of this exercise is to combat this pain and reduce the negative impact of these backhanded and double-edged comments.

NEXT STEPS

Provide clients with the **A Duck in the Rain** worksheet. Go over the backhanded comments with them, and ask them to identify some backhanded comments they heard growing up, or perhaps even comments they hear today from family members and/or significant others. Next, ask clients to rate how hurtful each comment is. Usually, the more hurtful the comment, the deeper the scars, and the more that clients repeat it over-and-over to themselves. For the last part of the exercise, have clients sit comfortably and go through the visualization exercise with them.

This exercise involves practicing a skill like any other, such that the more that your client does it, the better and more impactful it will be. This is not a "one and done" exercise. If your client likes the visualization, do it across several sessions and follow-up to see if they are using it in their everyday life.

A DUCK IN THE RAIN

A duck in the rain lets water roll off its back, and that is what this exercise is designed to help you do with all those backhanded comments you heard growing up. Individuals who grew up in homes with a parent or caregiver along the narcissistic spectrum are no strangers to backhanded and double-edged comments. On the surface, these comments can appear kind and helpful, but the reality is that they are wounds that leave scars. These comments hurt and create scars that echo throughout life and tend to increase in volume during times of stress.

Over time, they tear at your self-esteem and confidence. As an adult, you can make a choice to internalize those comments or to be a duck in the rain and let them roll off your back. This exercise is designed to help you build the skill to let those comments that reverberate in your mind roll off your back.

Comment	Translation
You look so healthy!	You look heavier than the last time I saw you.
You look good today. Are you doing something different?	You usually look a mess, and maybe you fixed it.
Did you do something different with your hair (skin, nails, other body part, etc.)? It looks so clean.	You are usually dirty and messy.
You finally got _____ fixed. Good for you.	Something was ugly about you previously, but you noticed it and finally fixed it.
You get better at your job/school everyday.	You are not very smart or good at what you do, but there may be hope for improvement.
All of your friends must feel safe being around you with their boyfriends.	You are unattractive, and no one would find you attractive.
There is someone out there for everyone, even you.	You are so defective, but someone may take pity on you and have a romantic relationship with you.
It's good you were finally able to get your _____ degree. A lot of people have that degree too, right?	It took you a long time because you're not smart or unique.
I didn't expect you to get that job. Congratulations.	I have low expectations of you and your achievements.
You certainly maximized your opportunities in college or at work.	You were promiscuous and wasted a valuable opportunity.
Not everyone is cut out for college.	You're not smart enough to earn a college degree.

Write down some of the backhanded comments you heard growing up and their accompanying translation. Rate the negative impact of each comment on a scale from 1 to 10 (1 = no negative impact; 10 = intense and long lasting impact).

Comment	Translation	Rating

The most hateful and hurtful comments (rated 7 or above) do not have to stick with you. Let those old comments and hurtful translations roll off, much like a duck in the rain lets water roll off its back. You can choose to act like a duck in the rain toward the comments that felt like a rainstorm all those years growing up, and perhaps even today. This is a great exercise in which to engage whenever those old comments and translations slip back into your mind. Become your duck, and let those comments roll off your back.

Follow the steps on the next page, and **be your duck**:

DUCK IN THE RAIN VISUALIZATION

1. **Imagine your duck with as much detail as you can.**

    a. How big is it? Some ducks are small, and some are large. It can be any size you want.

    b. What color are the feathers? There are yellow, white, black, and multicolored ducks. Any color is a good color.

    c. What do the head and beak look like? Is it a small, medium, large, or oversized head? Is it a long or short beak?

    d. What do your duck's feet look like? Small, medium, large? Subtle orange, bright orange, or another color?

2. **Where is your duck?**

    a. Inside your house, your parent or caregiver's house, your job, etc.? Maybe it is outside in a field, going down a sidewalk, etc.

3. **How are those backhanded comments falling?**

    a. Is it raining backhanded comments in large drops or many smaller drops?

    b. Even if you are indoors, it can rain through a sprinkler system or a dark cloud of backhanded comments hanging over you.

    c. See the words and phrases as rainfall.

4. **Now that you have a clear picture of your duck and surroundings, focus on the details of the duck and the environment.** See it clearly in your mind. Your duck is walking proudly, letting the comments and rainfall run off its back. Those old words and phrases do not stick; you do not internalize them. They slide off your back and onto the ground behind you. Perhaps they drain into the sewer if you are outside or seep into the floor inside your house or office. Your duck just keeps walking, letting all that rain slip off. Your duck is proud and confident, facing forward and being strong until the rain stops. You weathered the storm and came out proud, confident, and unscarred. You are a duck in the rain.

This is a great visualization exercise that can really help build the skills necessary to prevent these old comments from impacting you as much. With practice, this exercise will empower you to choose to internalize these comments or let them roll off your back. Many individuals who grew up in homes with parents or caregivers along the narcissistic spectrum believe that they are who they were told they are.

However, as adults, we have the power of choice, and that choice impacts your reality. Choosing to let those old backhanded and hurtful comments roll off your back will help you feel better about yourself and empower you to allow healthy and encouraging statements into your life. Make a habit of practicing this exercise so that when someone says a backhanded or hurtful comment, you and your duck are ready. The more you do this exercise, the more you will develop this skill and the greater its impact will be.

Digging Deeper into Motivations and Lessening Symptomatology

OVERCOMING THE 7 PAINS OF NARCISSISTIC PATHOLOGY

Individuals who grew up with a parent or caregiver along the narcissistic spectrum are likely to internalize the pathology and pain they experienced, causing it to become a part of their core structure (for more on core and surface structures, see Identifying Surface and Core Structures of Narcissistic Personality Disorder worksheet. Note: The concepts of core and surface structures are not specific to NPD and are not meant to indicate that your client falls along the narcissistic spectrum. Instead, the worksheet can be used to gain a greater understanding of the concept of core vs. surface structure). To create long-term change, the core structure needs to be addressed, and any underlying maladaptive and unhealthy symptomatology needs to be lessened. The 7 pains of narcissistic pathology are those factors that clients internalized from their developmental environment, which are listed and defined below.

Focusing on these 7 pains will not be easy, and defenses and resistance from your client are likely. However, to help clients overcome the hurt and pain they have experienced, or perhaps still experience, these must be addressed. The 7 techniques to overcoming the 7 pains are listed below as well. These 7 techniques can be utilized together or separately. The goal is to have clients use one, two, or as many of these techniques as possible, given that the more techniques that they use, the greater their ability to minimize and overcome the 7 pains. At first, these techniques will feel odd, forced, and foreign, but like any new skill, it becomes comfortable and habit-forming with practice.

NEXT STEPS

Go over the 7 pains of narcissistic pathology and the 7 techniques to overcome the 7 pains with your client. Make sure clients understand each one before asking them to complete the questions at the end. Encourage your client to be as concrete and descriptive as possible. Go over the results in session, and use the information to discuss each example and technique, as well as to illustrate how the techniques can be used in multiple situations and environments.

Most clients tend to see techniques as helpful in one situation, one environment, or with only one person. However, the following techniques can be impactful across all facets of your client's life. This is an activity that you will likely revisit multiple times and that can be used to illustrate therapeutic gains in your client. Maladaptive core structure is built up over years of pain and abuse, and it is not uncommon for it to take a year or more to overcome these maladaptive patterns and restructure the contents of the core structure.

OVERCOMING THE 7 PAINS OF NARCISSISTIC PATHOLOGY

Many individuals who grew up with parents or caregivers along the narcissistic spectrum are dealing with the 7 pains from their past that encourage maladaptive patterns and unhealthy choices.

By engaging in these patterns, you actually helped your parent or caregiver by giving him or her a sense of being "right about you all along." These patterns hurt your life and block you from moving forward. This activity is designed to help you move past them and into healthier and more adaptive patterns.

The 7 Pains of Narcissistic Pathology	
Emotional Fragility	Emotional fragility is feeling as though your emotions are always on edge. You are easily hurt by comments, misstatements, or the failure of others to do and say what you expect them to.
Indecisiveness	Indecisiveness involves difficulty settling on an issue or result and drawing a clear conclusion.
Self-Consciousness	Self-consciousness is feeling a heightened sense of attention or awareness regarding your appearance and actions.
Low self-trust	Low self-trust includes doubt and uncertainty regarding your ability to make decisions and ability to control and manage the consequences.
Fear of Successful Relationships	Fear of successful relationships is the distress you feel about losing something or ruining something that is good, hopeful, honest, and healing.
Impaired Self-Confidence	Impaired self-confidence includes uncertainty about your abilities and judgment.
Inhibition	Inhibition is the inability to be yourself in situations in a manner that is consistent with who you are and who you want to be.

7 techniques to overcome the 7 pains

1. **Act "as if" you are the opposite of your most impactful 7 pains.** Act "as if" you embrace good, hopeful, honest, and healing relationships, and trust that you deserve good things. Act this way and believe it, and eventually your brain and body will follow. You have to be willing to commit yourself to the idea of doing things differently.

2. **Communicate in a manner that encourages the opposite of the 7 pains.** Communicate in a manner with clear assertion and from the heart. Test the waters, and see how people respond when you remove your self-consciousness. Test your environment, and you'll be surprised that people respond in a positive manner. Those who do not may be the ones who benefit the most from your being self-conscious.

3. **Be willing to clear the clutter.** This step entails allowing people to self-select out of your life if they are not interested in you being the best and healthy version of yourself. When you choose to move away from the 7 pains, people who benefit from them are likely to want to keep you there. This is similar to the roles into which you fall when having a parent along the narcissistic spectrum (see Avoiding "The Family Crucible" Trap worksheet).

4. **Allow positive people to enter your life.** The 7 pains are good at preventing positive people from entering your life. Your top 3 pains are those that deflect positive people the most, but they do not have to.

5. **Have a determined heart.** The determined heart is one that is driven to succeed in a healthy manner. It is not deterred or distracted by the pathology of 7 pains, but plots a course of adaptive and healthy outcomes and refuses to fall back into old unhealthy patterns.

6. **Learn the steps to make it.** This technique includes building a knowledge base about yourself that will help you move forward and toward an adaptive and healthy lifestyle. Surround yourself with people from whom you can learn and who want to share what they know to help you grow, not to illustrate what you do not know. For example, parents or caregivers along the narcissistic spectrum tend to display knowledge so that others feel ignorant. In contrast, people who want to impart knowledge to help others want you to know what they know and want you to learn concepts and ideas to move you up and forward.

7. **Motion moves the ocean.** This step entails empowering yourself with movement and being an active participant to overcome the 7 pains. It involves not allowing yourself to stand still and take the abuse, but to move forward and create a force in your life so great that you move your ocean from unhealthy and maladaptive to healthy and adaptive.

Give an example of your emotional fragility: _____

_____

_____

Give an example of how you can use one or more of the 7 techniques to overcome the emotional fragility you learned from your parent or caregiver:

_____

_____

Give an example of your indecisiveness: _____

_____

_____

Give an example of how you can use one or more of the 7 techniques to overcome the indecisiveness you learned from your parent or caregiver: _____

_____

_____

Give an example of your self-consciousness: _____

_____

_____

Give an example of how you can use one or more of the 7 techniques to overcome the self-consciousness you learned from your parent or caregiver: _____

_____

_____

Give an example of your low self-trust: _____

_____

_____

Give an example of how you can use one or more of the 7 techniques to overcome the low self-trust you learned from your parent or caregiver: _____

_____

_____

Give an example of your fear of successful relationships: _____

_____

_____

Give an example of how you can use one or more of the 7 techniques to overcome the fear of successful relationships you learned from your parent or caregiver:

_____

_____

Give an example of your impaired self-confidence: _____

_____

_____

Give an example of how you can use one or more of the 7 techniques to overcome the impaired self-confidence you learned from your parent or caregiver: _____

_____

_____

Give an example of your inhibition: _____

_____

_____

Give an example of how you can use one or more of the 7 techniques to overcome the inhibition you learned from your parent or caregiver: _____

_____

_____

OVERCOMING THE DESTRUCTIVE INNER NARCISSISTIC FAMILY MEMBER

It is common for individuals who grew up with parents or caregivers along the narcissistic spectrum to have heard destructive, hurtful, and demeaning comments. Over time, these comments become internalized and part of the individuals' core structures. Getting to this part of the core structure is never easy, but asking clients to draw how they see this internalized maladaptive aspect can be a very powerful experience. This activity will allow you, the mental health provider, to see into your client's core structure and to address, confront, and reframe it. Keep in mind that resistance is likely whenever addressing core content, and be aware that reluctance to drawing is also common. However, recognizing and communicating the value in this experiential technique is very important in helping your client overcome the maladaptive impact of that destructive inner narcissistic family member.

NEXT STEPS

Provide your client with the **Overcoming the Destructive Inner Narcissistic Family Member** worksheet. Be sure to address concerns about artistic ability, and stress that this is not an artistic test, but a therapeutic tool to help address, confront, and reframe the source of old negative voices that have held the client back for a very long time. This activity can be done in session or as homework, and it can be used multiple times to mark changes as the impact of the destructive inner narcissistic family member decreases and your client's internal representation changes.

OVERCOMING THE DESTRUCTIVE INNER NARCISSISTIC FAMILY MEMBER

Many individuals who grew up with a parent or caregiver along the narcissistic spectrum heard destructive, hurtful, and demeaning comments growing up. Over time, these statements have become internalized and have echoed throughout your development and into your adult life. These statements encourage negative decision-making, which sets you up to justify the narcissistic family member's belief that your failure is his or her success. This concept is pleasing to the narcissistic family member because it proves that he or she was right, that you will never be successful, that you will never be happy, and that you do not deserve respect. This activity is designed to help you purge yourself of that destructive inner family member and move forward in an adaptive and healthy manner.

Draw your destructive inner narcissistic family member, and use the speech bubbles to write the statements that he or she made that have echoed throughout your life. This is not an art test, but an activity to free yourself from the bonds of narcissistic pathology. Do not be concerned with your artistic ability.

In the speech bubbles below, write the destructive inner voice statements that you identified in the exercise above. In the spaces provided to the right, provide evidence that proves that these statements are incorrect. Be as specific as you can in providing your evidence, and phrase it in as positive a manner as you can.

Evidence that proves my destructive inner voice is wrong:

_____

_____

_____

Evidence that proves my destructive inner voice is wrong:

_____

_____

_____

Evidence that proves my destructive inner voice is wrong:

_____

_____

_____

Now that you have evidence that the destructive inner voice is incorrect, draw yourself in the space below as you see yourself being free from the destructive, hurtful, and demeaning comments you heard growing up. Be sure that your speech bubbles are phrased positively, such as, "I am good at my job. I have gotten 3 promotions."

Save this picture, and refer back to it when/if the destructive inner narcissistic family member's voice comes back. You can update this picture as often as you would like as you continue to free yourself and put those destructive, hurtful, and demeaning comments farther behind you.

DIFFERENTIATION OF CHILD FROM PARENT

As children grow up, they internalize the values, beliefs, and views of their parents. Children with parents or caregivers along the narcissistic spectrum often see themselves through their parents' or caregivers' eyes and struggle because these values, beliefs, and views do not fit, are not helpful, and tend to lead to repetitive maladaptive patterns. Many clients with parents or caregivers along the narcissistic spectrum are aware of what has been instilled in them and how the pain associated with it affects how they feel about themselves and others. Although many have worked hard to do things differently with their children, romantic partners, friends, and coworkers, they still feel tethered to these maladaptive patterns.

This exercise is designed to help clients recognize those areas in which they exhibit different versus similar patterns as their parents or caregivers, as well as how to change these patterns, should they wish to do so. Continuing some of these characteristics may work for clients, whereas others are harmful and perpetuate their unhealthy view of themselves and the world. It is important to be aware of this duality and to discuss it with your client.

NEXT STEPS

Provide clients with the **Differentiation of Child from Parent** worksheet in session or as homework. The worksheet instructs clients to identify characteristics on which they are similar or different from their narcissistic parents or caregivers (called "comparison areas"). Ask clients to fill out the worksheet out, and go over their responses together. Focus on any successes they have made in differentiating themselves from their parents or caregivers, but also recognize the possible benefits of similarities (if clients are at a point where they can hear this).

You never want to seem like you are siding with a source of pain for your client. The last section of the activity is designed to challenge clients to find comparison areas that they would like to change and determine how they can change in these areas, as well as the benefits of that change. This can be a good activity for treatment planning and finding core content areas on which to focus.

DIFFERENTIATION OF CHILD FROM PARENT

Below is a list of characteristics on which you can compare and contrast yourself with your parent or caregiver along the narcissistic spectrum. Put a check mark on the chart whether you feel that you are similar to or different from your parent or caregiver along the narcissistic spectrum, and then describe these similarities and differences in the box.

If there is more than one characteristic that is not listed, you can use the back of the sheet. After completing the list, answer the questions at the end of the exercise to explore any comparison areas you would like to change, why you would like to change these areas, and how you are going to do so in order to help yourself. Work with your therapist to better understand your responses.

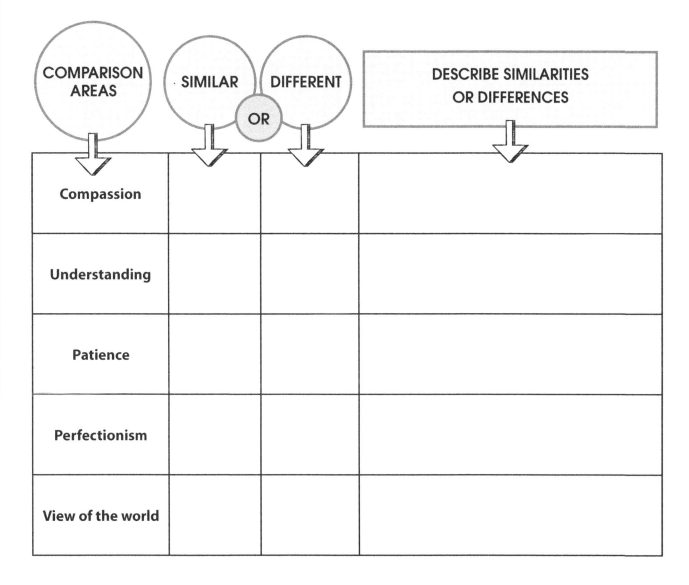

COMPARISON AREAS	SIMILAR	DIFFERENT	DESCRIBE SIMILARITIES OR DIFFERENCES
Compassion			
Understanding			
Patience			
Perfectionism			
View of the world			

COMPARISON AREAS	SIMILAR	DIFFERENT OR	DESCRIBE SIMILARITIES OR DIFFERENCES
Responsiblilty			
Anger			
Perservarance			
Outgoingness			
Reasoning			
Rule-consciousness			
Emotional stability			

Identify which comparison areas you would like to change and why: _____

_____

_____

Describe how you are going to change those areas to help yourself: _____

_____

_____

PARENTING DIFFERENTLY

Children of parents or caregivers along the narcissistic spectrum often internalize the manner in which they were parented. As they develop and notice the pain and difficulty that this has caused across various aspects of their lives (e.g., self-esteem, relationships, employment), they become driven to do things differently for themselves and their children. However, these individuals often respond to their own children in a default manner based on how they were raised, despite the fact that they want to parent differently in order for their children to grow up healthy, happy, and successful. The following guidelines listed are the 10 areas in which adult children of parents or caregivers along the narcissistic spectrum often have the greatest difficulty.

Learning new parenting skills is never easy because clients often feel torn between how they were taught to parent, how they want to parent, and how their children are developing. Mental health providers are excellent resources to encourage growth in parenting skills, and when success occurs, this is monumental proof that clients can do it differently for themselves and their children.

NEXT STEPS

Provide your client with the **Parenting Differently** worksheet. Go over each of the 10 guidelines, and assess the feasibility of adding these to your client's method of parenting. Some recommendations are going to be easier to implement than others, and based upon the ages of the children, the degree of resistance is variable. Discuss these topics with your client and start by implementing one or two of the guidelines. When the client has achieved success in one area, implement one or two more guidelines, and so on. Achieving a complete parenting overhaul is exceptionally difficult, and implementing one or two guidelines is a manageable task for success.

PARENTING DIFFERENTLY

Parenting is a learned skill, and many of us learned this skill by how we were parented. Individuals who grew up with parents or caregivers along the narcissistic spectrum tend to develop default tendencies to respond to others, even their children, based upon how they were raised. As a result, it is not uncommon to feel pulled in different directions because of how you were parented and how you want to parent. The 10 parenting guidelines listed below are difficulties that many children of parents or caregivers along the narcissistic spectrum experience when parenting their own children.

Use these 10 parenting guidelines to help you define your parenting style and to build new skills to break the cycle of narcissism for yourself and your children. After you have gone over the 10 guidelines, rank order them from least important to most important (1 = most important; 10 = least important) in terms of which guidelines you would like to implement first.

Belittling does little good.

Focus on the positive things that your child does, and you will start to see more positives. You may have grown up thinking that if you feel bad enough about yourself or something else, then you will decide to do good things. However, the truth is that if you always point out the negatives, you tend to lessen children's view of themselves and others, which creates a negative self-image.

Manners count.

Saying "please" and "thank you" to your children will encourage them to do the same to you and to others. Respect is a two-way street, and when you instill a sense of respect in your children, they internalize that and put that outward to others. In contrast, insulting and cursing at your children to have manners and be more polite is ineffective.

Model what you want your children to be.

Children learn from actions, not words. You may have grown up in a household where your parent or caregiver told you one thing but did something else, and if you ever questioned this, you were likely given the following explanation: "I am the adult/parent in charge here, you don't question me!" Doing it differently involves showing your children what you want them to aspire to. For example, if you want them to value education, then pursue education yourself – not necessarily by going to school, but by absorbing knowledge and having intellectual curiosity about things. In doing so, your child will develop these same values regarding education.

Parenting transparency.

Parenting is tough; patient and encouraging parenting is even harder. In an honest and respectful manner, let your children know that you are doing the best that you can for them. Doing so will encourage them to have compassion and empathy for you, their friends, and those around them. If you hide the challenges of parenting from your children and then blow up at them, this tends to encourage them to hide things from you and to do things behind your back.

Feelings matter.

Discuss your feelings with your children. Not about how they made you feel – because trying to make them feel guilty so they will do good things does not work – but how you feel about them. Respect their feelings, and they will return the gesture because they learned it from you. Never discount their feelings simply because they are children. Emotional responses are relative. For example, if your daughter's doll head falls off and she screams (common response), imagine if your good friend's head fell off. How would you feel?

Anger is better explained than expressed.

Everyone gets angry with his or her loved ones, and children are no exception. The key is to explain your anger and control it, instead of making children the direct recipients of your anger and causing collateral damage. When you are angry about something, it may or may not be a result of something that your children did. Make sure you think it through, and then explain your frustration in a manner that you would want someone to explain it to you. Children are easy targets for tirades of anger and rage, but how you display anger is a teaching method that you are sure to see repeated in the future. If you slip and blow up, then apologize, own it, and explain what you wish you had done differently.

Blame is not a game.

Blaming your children (e.g., for your feelings, if your plans were altered, etc.) only sends the message that they are at fault for your pain and inconvenience. Over time, children internalize the blame, which lowers their self-esteem, decreases their drive to succeed, and encourages co-dependency. If you were inconvenienced or your children failed to do something for which they were responsible, discuss the situation, possible negative consequences, and what they could have done differently. Blame is never a tool for learning.

You are the coach.

The best coaches are those who are patient and caring. Few people would ever say that the best coaches belittled them and made them feel small. Coaches who practice "tough love" with players (e.g., NFL, NBA, MLB, etc.) are more often supportive and encouraging than they are demeaning. This is because good coaches know that when you empower your players, then they perform. In contrast, when you demoralize them, they fail. Coach your kids to success with kindness, patience, appreciation, and understanding. If you do so with sincerity, then they will be sincere in return.

Mistakes, stumbles, and errors are great!

All children make mistakes, stumbles, and errors when they try new things or something does not go as planned. Fight the urge to make assumptions that your children did not know what they were doing (i.e., they are stupid) or they should have known (i.e., failure to plan ahead). Both of these assumptions are not helpful and tend to discourage children from taking appropriate risks because when they make mistakes, they will not seek you or anyone else out for guidance; they will just not take appropriate risks to begin with. The most successful people are those who take risks, stumble, get back up, and risk again. Be a source of encouragement for your children to try instead of being a source of ridicule.

Like your children.

Many parents or caregivers will demoralize, criticize, and disrespect their children right in front them. Doing so communicates a sense of dislike. Would you ever do that in front of your good friend? Most people would not. The most successful individuals on the planet can point back to a parent or caregiver who liked them. When we like our children, they are not a burden, a source to blame, or people who make your life miserable. Rather, they are people with whom you want to spend time and whose thoughts, fears, plans, and feelings you want to hear. Think of things that you like about your children and tell them frequently; they will love you for it.

Parenting is a skill. The more you practice these guidelines, the more you will build your parenting skills in these areas and the more you will see your children treat you and others differently. In the spaces below, rank order the guidelines based on how important they are to you and your children. Next, talk with your mental health provider about how to best implement the chosen guidelines into your parenting approach.

	Belittling does little good.
	Manners count.
	Model what you want your children to be.
	Parenting transparency.
	Feelings matter.
	Anger is better explained than expressed.
	Blame is not a game.
	You are the coach.
	Mistakes, stumbles, and errors are great!
	Like your children.

Final Steps

THE FAMILY DYNAMIC INFLUENCERS

When treating individuals with parents or caregivers along the narcissistic spectrum, family dynamics typically come up as critical issues to overcome and attenuate. The attached questionnaire is designed to help you and your client identify common issues related to family dynamics that are typically addressed throughout the course of treatment. This questionnaire can be given at various times throughout the treatment course to help with the therapeutic trajectory and to enhance clients' insights into the impact of treatment on their lives.

NEXT STEPS

Provide your client with **The Family Dynamic Influencers** worksheet in session or as homework. Go over the results together, and depending on whether the worksheet was given in the middle or at the end of treatment, explore the responses to determine if you need to (1) adjust the therapeutic trajectory or (2) provide some final coping skills and clarification about how and when your client may choose to resume treatment.

THE FAMILY DYNAMIC INFLUENCERS

Identify the impact that treatment has had on the following family dynamic influencers. Answer each question as it affects you and your life today. After rating the 15 family dynamic influencers, answer the questions at the end of this worksheet to help you gain greater insight and awareness going forward, either while you are still in treatment or upon its completion.

1. How comfortable I am with myself.

①	②	③	④	⑤
Much Better	Somewhat Better	Stayed The Same	Somewhat Worse	Much Worse

2. My parent's/caregiver's relationship with me.

①	②	③	④	⑤
Much Better	Somewhat Better	Stayed The Same	Somewhat Worse	Much Worse

3. How my parent/caregiver treats my sibling(s) as compared to me.

①	②	③	④	⑤
Much Better	Somewhat Better	Stayed The Same	Somewhat Worse	Much Worse

4. Family of origin values, culture, beliefs, and views.

①	②	③	④	⑤
Much Better	Somewhat Better	Stayed The Same	Somewhat Worse	Much Worse

5. How safe and secure I feel with my parent/caregiver.

①	②	③	④	⑤
Much Better	Somewhat Better	Stayed The Same	Somewhat Worse	Much Worse

6. How confident I feel about myself.

①	②	③	④	⑤
Much Better	Somewhat Better	Stayed The Same	Somewhat Worse	Much Worse

7. My level of anxiety.

①	②	③	④	⑤
Much Better	Somewhat Better	Stayed The Same	Somewhat Worse	Much Worse

8. My level of depression.

①	②	③	④	⑤
Much Better	Somewhat Better	Stayed The Same	Somewhat Worse	Much Worse

9. My self-esteem.

①	②	③	④	⑤
Much Better	Somewhat Better	Stayed The Same	Somewhat Worse	Much Worse

10. My ability to be social.

①	②	③	④	⑤
Much Better	Somewhat Better	Stayed The Same	Somewhat Worse	Much Worse

11. My ability to be myself.

①	②	③	④	⑤
Much Better	Somewhat Better	Stayed The Same	Somewhat Worse	Much Worse

12. My ability to be fair with myself.

①	②	③	④	⑤
Much Better	Somewhat Better	Stayed The Same	Somewhat Worse	Much Worse

13. My satisfaction with my life.

   ①   ②   ③   ④   ⑤

Much Better	Somewhat Better	Stayed The Same	Somewhat Worse	Much Worse

14. My hope to do things differently.

   ①   ②   ③   ④   ⑤

Much Better	Somewhat Better	Stayed The Same	Somewhat Worse	Much Worse

15. My ability to choose the future I want and to choose what is best for me.

   ①   ②   ③   ④   ⑤

Much Better	Somewhat Better	Stayed The Same	Somewhat Worse	Much Worse

What was it about the treatment process that made you mark any items as "(1) Much Better" or "(2) Somewhat Better"? Be as descriptive as possible: _____

_____

_____

_____

What changes will you implement going forward to sustain your gains?

_____

_____

_____

What was it about the treatment process that made you mark any items as "(4) Somewhat Worse" or "(5) Much Worse"? Be as descriptive as possible: _____

_____

_____

_____

What would you like to change going forward to prevent those items you marked as "(4) Somewhat Worse" or "(5) Much Worse" from becoming worse? _____

_____

_____

_____

THERAPEUTIC MILESTONES

When clients reach points of success in treatment and overcome the hurt and pain that have created maladaptive and unhealthy patterns, we should log these successes so clients can see the changes they have made. This exercise can be used with any client – not just those who are along the narcissistic spectrum or who are a partner or child of someone along the narcissistic spectrum. Logging successes is critical, and this exercise is designed to help clients clearly recognize the gains they have made in areas that are most commonly impaired by narcissistic spectrum pathology. Many mental health providers mistakenly believe that clients will inherently remember the milestones they have made in treatment, but when clients are finished with treatment, there is typically a degree of regression that takes place. This exercise is designed to stall or prevent that regression.

NEXT STEPS

Provide clients with the **Therapeutic Milestones** worksheet, and ask them to complete it in session or as homework. Be sure to tell clients that not everyone achieves milestones in every domain, that most clients do not have concerns in all domains, and that they should focus on the domains in which they reached therapeutic milestones. This is an exercise where the mental health provider is a cheerleader for clients; shower them with encouragement and praise. If you are giving clients this exercise, then they have earned it. ☺

THERAPEUTIC MILESTONES

When you learn how to replace maladaptive and unhealthy patterns associated with narcissistic pathology with healthy and adaptive patterns, you have changed the course of your life. Below are two therapeutic milestone logs for you to write out the successes you have made in treatment. Milestones are those successes that have changed your life in the areas identified below. The first log is intended for milestones as they relate to you and others (relationships and family), whereas the second log specifically relates to you and areas of growth that you have had.

There are also blank spaces left at the end of each log so you can write down any milestone categories not included here. Write your successes out in as much detail as possible, and try to phrase them in as positive a manner as you can.

Therapeutic Milestone Log – Self and Others	
Personal	
Relationship	
Family	
Other milestones:	

Therapeutic Milestone Log - Self	
Communication	
Stress Reduction	
Building relationships	
Self-esteem	
Self-appreciation	
Giving and receiving positive attention	
Giving and receiving negative attention	
Degree to which I feel heard	
Other milestones:	

References

For your convenience, purchasers can download and print
worksheets and handouts from www.pesi.com/NPD

American Psychiatric Association. (2013). *Diagnostic and statistical manual of mental disorders*. 5th ed. Washington, DC: Author.

Benjamin, L.S. (1996). *Interpersonal diagnosis and treatment and personality disorders*. 2nd ed. New York, NY: Guilford Press.

Bernard, M.E. and Ellis, A. (2011). *Clinical applications of rational-emotive therapy*. New York, NY: Springer.

Besser, A., and Priel, B. (2009). Emotional responses to a romantic partner's imaginary rejection: The roles of attachment anxiety, covert narcissism, and self-evaluation. *Journal of Personality*, 77(1), pp. 287–325.

Bowlby, J. (1988). *A secure base: Parent–child attachment and healthy human development*. New York, NY: Basic Books.

Brailovskaia, J., and Bierhoff, H. (2016). Cross-cultural narcissism on Facebook: Relationship between self-presentation, social interaction and the open and covert narcissism on a social networking site in Germany and Russia. *Computers in Human Behavior*, 55, pp. 251–257.

Bushman, B.J., and Baumeister, R.F. (1998). Threatened egotism, narcissism, self-esteem, and direct and displaced aggression: Does self-love or self-hate lead to violence? *Journal of Personality and Social Psychology*, 75(1), pp. 219–229.

Deci, E.L., and Ryan, R.M. (1985). *Intrinsic motivation and self-determination in human behavior*. New York, NY: Plenum.

Deci, E.L., and Ryan, R.M. (2000). The "what" and "why" of goal pursuits: Human needs and the self-determination of behavior. *Psychological Inquiry*, 11(4), pp. 227–268.

Donaldson-Pressman, S., and Pressman, R.M. (1994). *The narcissistic family: Diagnosis and treatment*. San Francisco, CA: Jossey-Bass Publishers.

Forward, S., and Frazier, D. (1998). *Emotional blackmail: When the people in your life use fear, obligation, and guilt to manipulate you*. New York, NY: Harper Collins.

Fox, D. (2013). *The clinician's guide to the diagnosis and treatment of personality disorders*. Eau Claire, WI: PESI Publishing and Media.

Gilligan, J. (1996). *Violence: Our deadly epidemic and its causes*. New York, NY: G.P. Putnam's Sons.

Gunderson, J.G., and Ronningstam, E. (2001). Differentiating narcissistic and antisocial personality disorders. *Journal of Personality Disorders*, 15(2), 103–109.

Kernberg, O.F. (1998). Pathological narcissism and narcissistic personality disorder: Theoretical background and diagnostic classification. In: E.F. Ronningstam, ed., *Disorders of Narcissism:*

Diagnostic, Clinical, and Empirical Implications. Arlington, VA: American Psychiatric Association, pp. 29–51.

Kohut, H. (1971). *The analysis of the self: A systematic approach to the psychoanalytic treatment of narcissistic personality disorders.* New York, NY: International Universities Press.

Livesley, W.J. (2007). A framework for integrating dimensional and categorical classifications of personality disorder. *Journal of Personality Disorders, 21*(2), pp. 199–224.

McBride, K. (2008). *Will I ever be good enough? Healing the daughters of narcissistic mothers.* New York, NY: Atria Paperback.

Ronningstam, E.F. (1999). Narcissistic personality disorder. In: T. Millon, P.H. Blaney, & R.D. Davis, eds., *Oxford Textbook of Psychopathology.* New York, NY: Oxford University Press, pp. 674–693.

Ronningstam, E.F. (2011). Narcissistic personality disorder in DSM V – In support of retaining a significant diagnosis. *Journal of Personality Disorders, 25*(2), 248–259.

Rose, P. (2002). The happy and unhappy faces of narcissism. *Personality and Individual Differences, 33,* pp. 379–392.

Ryan, R.M. and Deci, E.L. (2000). Self-determination theory and the facilitation of intrinsic motivation, social development, and well-being. *American Psychologist, 55*(1), pp. 68–78.

Tellegen, A. and Waller, N.G. (2008). Exploring personality through test construction: Development of the Multidimensional Personality Questionnaire. In: G. Boyle, G. Matthews, & D. Saklofske, eds., *The SAGE Handbook of Personality Theory and Assessment,* Vol 2. London: SAGE Publications Ltd., pp. 261–292.

Widiger, T.A. (2006). Psychopathy and DSM-IV psychopathology. In: C.J. Patrick, ed., *Handbook of Psychopathy.* New York, NY: Guilford Press, pp. 156–171.

Wink, P. (1991). Two faces of narcissism. *Journal of Personality and Social Psychology, 61*(4), pp. 590–597.

World Health Organization. (2016). *The ICD-10 classification of mental and behavioural disorders: Clinical descriptions and diagnostic guidelines.* Geneva: World Health Organization.

Zondag, H.J. (2005). Between imposing one's will and protecting oneself: Narcissism and the meaning of life among Dutch pastors. *Journal of Religion and Health, 44,* pp. 413–426.